Christian Contemplation

Christian Contemplation

Theological Foundations and Contemporary Practice

JOSEPH H. NGUYEN, SJ

WIPF & STOCK · Eugene, Oregon

CHRISTIAN CONTEMPLATION
Theological Foundations and Contemporary Practice

Copyright © 2020 Joseph H. Nguyen. All rights reserved. Except for brief quotations in critical publications or reviews, no part of this book may be reproduced in any manner without prior written permission from the publisher. Write: Permissions, Wipf and Stock Publishers, 199 W. 8th Ave., Suite 3, Eugene, OR 97401.

Wipf & Stock
An Imprint of Wipf and Stock Publishers
199 W. 8th Ave., Suite 3
Eugene, OR 97401

www.wipfandstock.com

PAPERBACK ISBN: 978-1-7252-8669-6
HARDCOVER ISBN: 978-1-7252-8668-9
EBOOK ISBN: 978-1-7252-8673-3

Manufactured in the U.S.A.   10/26/20

Contents

Preface		vii
Introduction		ix
Chapter 1	Contemplative Prayer	1
Chapter 2	Spiritual Discernment in the Contemplative Life	30
Chapter 3	Jesus Christ in the Contemplative Life	61
Conclusion		87
Bibliography		99

Preface

THE MAIN IDEA CONTAINED in this book comes from the conversations I had with Dr. Eric Cunningham, Professor of History at Gonzaga University. We were both interested in the art of contemplation. The question that arose from our conversations was: How can the ancient art of contemplation help us cultivate spiritual depth amidst the hectic life of the fast-paced and consumerist society in which we live? Being well-versed in Zen Buddhism, Dr. Cunningham provided some insights from Zen Buddhist practitioners, highlighting the importance of meditation as an effective way to awaken one to the spiritual self. We both observed some similarities between Buddhist meditation and Christian contemplation, in particular with regard to their meditative methods. The *Jesus Prayer*, one of the most ancient Christian prayers, for example, insists on the need to pay close attention to one's own breathing and to bring one's mind and heart into unison in prayer. This is exactly what a Zen Buddhist practitioner attempts to achieve. Thus, we observed that both Buddhist meditation and Christian contemplation aim to waken the self to the spiritual realm through deep breathing. However, we also recognized the differences between the doctrinal points of view of the two traditions. Buddhism and Christianity are grounded on two distinct religious traditions.

The objective of this book does not aim to compare and contrast Buddhist meditation to Christian contemplation. The main goal of the book is to present and explain the nature and function of Christian contemplation from its theological foundations and contemporary practice, and to make Christian contemplation compelling and relevant to contemporary readers.

I am well aware of the fact that many today have already been exposed to meditative techniques such as *spiritual yoga* and *centering prayer*. Yoga practitioners and those who pray using centering prayer method will find points of contact in the *Jesus Prayer* represented in this book. It is for this reason that the general readers I intended are spiritual seekers, Christian and non-Christian alike, who are interested in the search for spiritual depth in their lives. However, being a Jesuit Catholic priest and a college professor of Christian spirituality, I intended to write this book as an academic book useable in the classroom whose main readers are undergraduate students and their professors.

A few words about the essential theme of the book must now be provided. From the Christian perspective, true prayer comes from the Holy Spirit. That is, when we are disposed to the Holy Spirit from within our heart in contemplation, it is then the Holy Spirit who prays in us rather than we ourselves who pray, for as Saint Paul says, "For we do not know how to pray as we ought, but that very Spirit intercedes for us with sighs too deep for words" (Romans 8:26). The central aim of Christian contemplation, therefore, is union with God, and true contemplation is the work of the Holy Spirit. This is the main theme addressed in the present book.

I would like to thank Dr. Cunningham for his valuable conversations from which the original idea of this book came. The present book would not have come to the final form without the help of two brother Jesuits of mine: Fathers Jim Torrens, SJ and Father Tim Clancy, SJ. Father Clancy is an Associate Professor of Philosophy at Gonzaga University. He read the entire manuscript of the book and gave observations and comments that enabled me to revise the book and make it a fuller and more accessible to the reader. Father Torrens is a writer in residence at the Della Strada Jesuit Community in Spokane, Washington. His editing skills and calm approach to writing helped me to clarify ideas and expressions with more precision. Finally, I would like to thank Cascade Books who accepted my book for publication.

JOSEPH H. NGUYEN, SJ
SAN FRANCISCO
FEAST OF SAINT IGNATIUS OF LOYOLA, 2020

Introduction

IN THE FAST-PACED AND consumerist society in which we live, many people move through the day without being aware of a need to pause and reflect on the meaning and purpose of life. But without reflection one cannot be conscious of his or her deep desire in life; and without the knowledge of a deeper desire of the heart, one cannot find satisfaction in life because the heart only satisfied when its deeper desires are met.

Contemplation can play a role in the search for these human deeper desires. But many will ask: does contemplation still exist? If one has been led to believe that there indeed exists the art of contemplation, one will still perhaps wonder what it is and whether or not it is still relevant and applicable today. For many, the term "contemplation" itself perhaps connotes a sense of an exotic practice from a distant past unrelated and impractical to the contemporary life.

But for those who are more in tune with the need for a well-balanced approach to life, meditation has proved to be effective. One only needs to observe how many people have taken up the practice of yoga today. One can practically find a yoga class in most cities in the United States. Isn't it true that yoga classes are popular because people have found that yoga meditation helps them to cope with their hectic lives in our world today?

So, on the one hand, since the desire for a healthier lifestyle has led many to take up the practice of yoga; that should indicate to us that they are aware of the need to counter a fast-paced and consumerist way of life that has influenced us negatively. But, on the other hand, yoga classes are not enough! The human desire for contentment will not stop short at a mere peaceful and balanced lifestyle. From the Christian point of view, the human soul is created by God and keeps yearning for its Creator. Nothing in the created world can satisfy the desire of the soul. No wonder many people have searched for the object of their heart's desire in material things only to realize that their deeper desires are not satisfied. Practicing yoga is a good start in the search for true peace, but one must invest in Christian contemplation for a different kind of nourishment; that is, for divine union.

True contemplation differs from any meditative method in that the Christian contemplative finds union with God not only for himself or herself, but also for other human beings. There is a communal dimension in Christian contemplation that searches for God in all of God's creatures, especially in the poor, the marginalized and the oppressed. Seen from this perspective, Christian contemplation can offer people a new way to search for the self: a self in communion with God and with each other.

In the following pages, I will explore the nature and function of Christian contemplation and offer the reader a wide variety of contemplative prayer methods that can help cultivate an awareness of the spiritual dimension of the human life. The discussion will be grounded in the Christian anthropological theological foundations, which asserts that human beings are created for the purpose of union with God. From this foundational theological view, a number of questions can and should be raised: How is divine union possible? What are the conditions for divine union? And what is divine union for? In regard to the art of contemplation, additional questions can also be raised. Examples may include the following: What is the object of contemplation? How does one contemplate? And what is the end-result of contemplation? All these are questions relevant to the topic of Christian contemplation; and the reader will hopefully find the answers to them in the following pages.

The first chapter will present and discuss the nature and function of Christian contemplation by tracing its roots in ancient philosophical and spiritual traditions. The chapter will, then, explore subsequent developments of contemplation in the Christian tradition from ancient times to contemporary contexts. Clearly, such an attempt will not allow for an in-depth study of each of the particular developments within this evolution of Christian contemplation. Nonetheless, attempts will be made to accentuate the central development within each movement and to expound similarities and differences in comparison to the previous developments. In doing so, the chapter will highlight the characteristic features that are common to all developments and underscore the essence of Christian contemplation and its function in the Christian life.

The second chapter will address the relationship between contemplation and spiritual discernment. Divine union, which is the final end of contemplation, can be appropriated through human experience of the divine. But how does one discern this experience of God? This is the overall concern of the chapter. The chapter will begin by tracing the origin of the term "spiritual discernment" by exploring its usage in Scripture, particularly in the letters of Saint Paul. Grounding itself in the Scriptural understanding of spiritual discernment, the chapter will then explore how the early Church monastic tradition understood and practiced it. The last part of the chapter will present and explain some of the essential rules for the discernment of spirits in the *Spiritual Exercises* of Saint Ignatius of Loyola (1491–1556).

No one can deny that the distinctive characteristic feature of Christian contemplation is grounded in the Person of Jesus Christ, the Incarnation of God. The third and last chapter, therefore, will study the nature and role of Christ in contemplation.

The theology of the Incarnation implies that in Jesus the divine reality and the human reality have been completely united. That is, in Jesus Christ, God has been fully manifest to the world and human beings can hope that they, too, can live lives in union with Christ and thus reach their highest potential through divine union.

The first part of the chapter will explore this theological anthropology from the theology of the Incarnation, highlighting the human capability for self-transcendence in Christ. The chapter will study the transcendental theology of Bernard Lonergan (1904–1984) and interpret the *Spiritual Exercises* of Saint Ignatius (1491–1556) through Lonergan's transcendental method. The chapter will, then, reinterpret the answers to the questions raised at the beginning of this introduction. These are: How is divine union possible? What are the conditions for divine union? And what is divine union for? The second part of the chapter will employ Lonergan's transcendental method to interpret the *Spiritual Exercises* of Saint Ignatius, centering on the Ignatian understanding of Contemplation in Action. Thus, the second part will attempt to answer the questions raised earlier regarding contemplation. These are: What is the object of contemplation? How does one contemplate? And what is the end-result of contemplation?

Chapter 1

Contemplative Prayer

A COMMON UNDERSTANDING OF PRAYER

WHAT IS PRAYER? AND why do Christians pray? At first glance, these questions seem to be redundant, because many Christians will claim that they already know what prayer is and why they pray. Many practicing Catholics, for example, say the Rosary commemorating the mysteries of the Christian faith exemplified in the life of Mary, the Mother of God. Attending Mass on Sundays and other days of the week as their circumstances permit is another way to pray collectively. The Catholic Mass is the highest form of communal prayer, one that expresses the human encounter of the divine in thanksgiving. Even non-practicing Christians, on occasion, pray for peace and justice, or for the needs and intentions of others, or in grief at the loss of a loved one.

So, speaking in a broad sense, Christians in general and Catholics in particular do pray, either regularly or on occasion; and they do so in various ways according to their needs and circumstances. Some praise and thank God for the blessings they have received. Others ask God for the forgiveness of their own sin and for deliverance from temptation to sin. Many pray for the grace to let go of their own grudges and resentments towards others whom they find it difficult to forgive or from whom they wish forgiveness. Last but not least, many Christians pray for the needs and intentions of others, especially in times of suffering and hardship. These forms of prayer and their variations are effective ways to communicate to a good and living God who in Jesus manifests unconditional love and mercy for humanity and for the rest of creation.

But the question can be raised: What happens when one is not praying, for one cannot pray all the time? This is not a trivial question in our present context of the falling off of prayer so common among Christians. Practicing Catholics, for example, go to church on Sundays to pray and worship together for about an hour at Mass; but not many will return to the sacrament of the Eucharist during the week, nor pray in some form regularly. The reason for this lack of prayer varies from person to person often due to life circumstances. Whatever the reason, Christians should not excuse themselves from prayer which in an essential way to help one to deepen relationship with God and cultivate a better understanding of his or her own identity in relation to the divine.

A BRIEF NOTE ON THE TERMINOLOGY OF CONTEMPLATION

To pray effectively, and so to conceive better of prayer than is described above, it helps to explore briefly a mode of prayer traditionally called "contemplation." In the Christian tradition, the term "contemplation" signifies the highest form of prayer, and is described as "the summit of all prayers." The word "contemplation" originates in the Latin word, *templum* (sacred space), a diminutive of *tempus* (time). In Ancient Rome, the Romans employed *tempus* to signify "a division or section of time" and to mark off a sacred space (*templum*) from other spaces thereby allowing approved spiritual readers to examine sacred texts and to reveal their meanings to listeners.[1] As one can see from this usage, *contemplation* means to listen carefully to the sacred texts so as to discern their meanings.

Another source for the meaning of the English word "contemplation" is the Greek word *theōria*, often mistranslated into English as "theory." This literal translation does not reflect the original meaning of *theōria*. The English word "theory" often denotes a conceptual postulate, which may or may not have been tested or realized in practice. The Greek *theōria* does not convey this meaning. Rather *theōria* means "to look at something intently and for a purpose."[2] In other words, *theōria* signifies a contemplative state of mind able to discern and recognize the essence of things beyond their appearance.

1. Downey, *New Dictionary*, 209.
2. Downey, *New Dictionary*, 210.

The Greek Fathers of the early Church employed the term *theōria* in their ascetical writings to construct and explain the highest state of contemplation, whereby the human soul is capable of discerning the essence of created realities and to perceive them as coming from God. The Fathers believed that human beings were created in the image and likeness of God for the purpose of union with God. The human soul, though created with the body, has innate capacity for the spiritual realm beyond the physical. In this view, the soul is the essence of the human being, but the soul does not exist apart from nor is it independent of the body. Contemplation is the mode of prayer that awakens the soul to its highest and most noble existence whereby the person is capable for union with God, and through this divine union, can live in harmony with others.

The Latin word *contemplatio*, from which the English word "contemplation" takes its form, was used by the early Church Fathers of the Latin West to translate the term *theōria* from the Greek ascetical writings. Seen from the terminological point of view, the Latin *contemplatio* conveys the similar meaning and function as the Greek *theōria*. Thus, to summarize in one statement, we can say that the English word *contemplation* really means to meditate on the word of God in the scriptures for the purpose of seeing the created realities from the divine.

In the development of Christian contemplation there have been two main tendencies generally characterized as an "intellectual spirituality" and a "heart spirituality." The key figure in the development of an "intellectual spirituality" is Evagrius Ponticus (345–99). He develops the three stages of spiritual growth called *practical*, *natural*, and *theological* stages. For example, Evagrius instructs, "Pray first for purification of the passions; secondly for deliverance from ignorance and forgetfulness; and thirdly, for deliverance from all temptation and dereliction" (*On Prayer*, 38).[3] Each stage aims to produce a desirable result. In the first stage, the goal is to purify the soul from the base reality absorbed by the bodily senses and to attain *agape* (or disinterested love); the second stage aims at the understanding of the order of the created world by freeing the mind from the ignorance of the essence of created things; in the final stage, the soul, which has now been purified and enlightened, and is able to unite with the divine spirit spontaneously. For Evagrius, the three stages of spiritual growth relate to each other in an essentially way; the higher stage depends on the lower one and completes the lower one. The contemplative (the one who prays using this method), cannot move to the higher stage of prayer until he or she has completed the lower stage; the higher stage, once achieved, will produce the condition in which

---

3. Kadloubovsky and Palmer, *Philokalia*, 60.

the lower stage can be realized and practiced spontaneously. The advantage of this method of contemplation can be seen in the fact that it is orderly; that is, structured with a clear objective for each stage of the prayer as well as its final goal. The disadvantage of this type of prayer method is that it construes contemplation as essentially an activity of the mind, or the intellect, resulting in the split between mind and body. The final goal of contemplation, for Evagrius, is to achieve the state of the mind whereby the human mind completely unites with the mind of God in an immaterial manner.[4]

The other tendency develops prayer as essentially coming from the heart. For this reason, the second tendency is often distinguished from the first method by the name "heart spirituality." Representative of this tradition was Macarius (300–390). Unlike Evagrius, who construes contemplation as essentially taking place in the mind, Macarius conceives contemplation as essentially an activity of the heart. In this view, the heart, having been uprooted of its evil intentions, can increasingly come to the awareness of God's spirit from within and can even encounter the presence of the indwelling of the Trinity.[5]

THE PRAYER OF THE HEART

The prayer of the heart associates with the "heart spirituality" tradition developed by Macarius. In the Christian spiritual tradition, this prayer is based on the inspiration of two particular scriptural texts: Psalm 51 and Matthew 15. The passage from Matthew 15:10–20 contains the teaching of Jesus about the importance of the intention of the heart and why the heart's intention needs to be pure. Jesus says, "It is not what goes into the mouth that defile a person, but it is what comes out of the mouth that defines" (Matt 15:11).[6] The reason for this is that what comes out of the mouth, i.e., what one speaks, proceeds from the intention of the heart and is conditioned by that intention (Matt 15:17). Thus, if the heart's intention is not pure, then what one speaks, chooses and acts out will also be impure.

Note the emphasis Jesus puts on the interior disposition, that is, of the intention of the will over against the observation of external appearances. Things in the physical world occur and can affect us positively or negatively, but they happen to us, and in most cases we do not have control over their occurrences. What we can and should do is to judge the appearances of

---

4. See Nguyen, *Apatheia in the Christian Tradition*, 8–18.

5. Maloney, *Prayer of the Heart*, 20.

6. New Revised Standard Version (NRSV), 1989. Thereafter, all biblical citations will be taken from this version.

things; and this we do by reflecting on them, evaluating their results, and discerning a way in which we deal with them. The process of reflecting, evaluating and discerning does not come about merely by the activity of the mind; the heart must be involved. The heart, in a sense, is the seat of judgment. It is the center of the personality where the person can perceive things in a whole and integral way.

The psalmist was one to have realized the necessity for a pure heart, capable of discerning the good from the bad, the holy from the profane and the life-giving from the life-destroying. The psalmist cries out, "Create in me a clean heart, O God, and put a new and right spirit within me" (Ps 51:10). He knows that only the heart created anew in God's Spirit can be in tune with that Spirit. Apart from the Spirit of God, the human heart simply does not know how to pray to God as it should. True prayer is a work of the Holy Spirit.

The *prayer of the heart* should be conceived from this point of view; that is, it is the expression of God's Spirit in the human heart. Perhaps that is why the *prayer* is often conceived as the summit of all prayers. The *prayer* expresses the deepest desire of the human heart, the desire to be united with the Spirit of God, a desire that can only be attained when the heart is pure. Theologians have distinguished two different but interrelated goals for the *prayer of the heart*. The *immediate goal* is to achieve the purity of heart, a heart free from evil intentions and thus, capable of listening to God's Spirit. The *final goal* is the union with God, a union that can only be attained when the human heart is capable of listening attentively to God's Spirit.

Seen from the point of view of the divine-human interaction, the whole process of the *prayer of the heart* begins with God and ends in God. Even the human desire for a pure heart, which is subjectively perceived as something coming from the person's heart, in fact comes from God. If it were not God's own Spirit inspiring the person to desire for a pure heart, the person would not be able to have such a desire, for an impure heart cannot produce a holy desire. But before the desire for the pure heart can be realized as coming from God, the person must have experienced a contrary condition of his or her own heart. This could be the condition that generates anxiety, disharmony and discontentment, or any other negative feelings. Like the psalmist who cries out to God for help, the person experiencing anxiety, disharmony and discontentment in her heart, cries out, "Create a clean heart in me, O God, and put a new and right spirit within me" (Ps 51:10). The condition for that conversion of the desire of the heart must come from the divine source. The *prayer of the heart* evokes in the contemplative a capability to realize his or her need for God on the one hand and creates a condition in which he or she can readily receive God's Spirit on the other hand. The *prayer* prepares the contemplative to listen to God's Spirit from within his or her heart. The whole process starts and ends with God and in God. All the contemplative can do is to dispose himself or herself to the working of the Holy Spirit.

Our contemporary situation presents an unfortunate phenomenon. We are accustomed to approaching prayer as something we do, an initiative of ours; we do not know how to pray as we should. The *prayer of the heart*, unlike other prayers, teaches us that true prayer is the work of the Holy Spirit. It is the Spirit who prays in us. As Saint Paul says, "The Spirit helps us in our weakness; for we do not know how to pray as we ought, but that very Spirit intercedes with sighs too deep for words. And God, who searches the heart, knows what is the mind of the Spirit, because the Spirit intercedes for the saints according to the will of God" (Rom 8:26–27).

THE JESUS PRAYER

It is from the tradition of the *prayer of the heart* that the *Jesus prayer* was developed. The instruction for the *Jesus prayer* is very simple. The prayer consists of two parts. First the person calls on the name of Jesus by saying, "Lord Jesus Christ, Son of the Living God." Then one asks for mercy by uttering the words, "have mercy on me, a sinner." Thus the whole prayer can be said in one breath. In the breathing-in, one says, "Lord Jesus Christ, Son of the Living God;" and in the breathing-out, one says, "have mercy on me, a sinner."

John Meyendorff, a scholar in Orthodox spirituality, describes Macarius' instruction on the *Jesus prayer* in the following words, "There is no need to waste time with words; it is enough to hold out your hands and say: Lord, according to your desire and to your wisdom, have mercy. If you are hard pressed in the struggle, say: Lord save me! He knows what is best for you, and he will have mercy on you."[7]

Specific instructions on how to prepare one's self for the *Jesus prayer* and on what to do with distractions during the *prayer* can be taken from Saint Simeon the New Theologian (949–1022), cited in *The Way of a Pilgrim*. *The Way of a Pilgrim* is a little book composed by a Russian pilgrim whose name remains unknown. In it, the author tells stories of how he has learned the *Jesus prayer* from an elder priest. The first instruction explains the general preparation for the *prayer*. It goes as follows:

> Bend your head, close your eyes, and breathe softly. In your imagination, look into your own heart. Let your mind, or rather,

---

7. Meyendorff, *Saint Gregory Palamas and Orthodox Spirituality*, 18.

your thoughts, flow from your head down to your heart and say, while breathing: "Lord Jesus Christ, have mercy on me." Whisper these words gently, or say them in your mind. Discard all other thoughts. Be serene, persevering and repeat them over and over again.[8]

One can observe that the essential thing here is to acquire the habit of making the mind stand in guard of the heart. The contemplative imagines that all thoughts from his mind flow down to the heart and join to the heart in this prayer. This is why the *Jesus prayer* can also be called a *mind-in-heart prayer*. It is also important to remember that the success of this prayer does not come about by mere human effort; it is the work of grace. Perhaps the sincere attitude one should have in this prayer is one of humility in recognizing the need for God's mercy, and a desire to be united with God's Spirit.[9]

The *Jesus prayer* can be said in most circumstances and in various positions. One can say the prayer while sitting, standing or walking. The prayer can be shortened as one continues praying. For example, the full prayer, "Lord Jesus, Son of the Living God, have mercy on me, a sinner" can be said in shorter version, "Jesus, have mercy on me." In this prayer, the words are not as important as the breathing itself. In the breathing-in and breathing-out continuously with the intention to bring the mind down to the heart to join the heart in this prayer, one eventually prays silently with one's own breath.

The described instruction sounds simple, but many monks who practice the *Jesus prayer* have learned that it is difficult to control one's flow of thoughts during the prayer. They know from experience that it isn't the external distractions as much as one's own thoughts that can prevent one from praying constantly. The following instruction from Nicephorus the Solitary proves to be helpful on how to guard the intention of the heart from distracting thoughts:

> If, however, in spite of all your efforts, you do not succeed in entering into the realm of the heart, as I have described, do what I shall now tell you and, with God's help, you will find what you seek. You know that in every person, inner talking is in the breast. For, when our lips are silent, it is in the breast that we talk and discourse with ourselves, pray and sing psalms, and do other things. Thus, having banished every thought from this inner talking (for you can do this if you want), give it the following short prayer: "Lord, Jesus Christ, Son of God, have

---

8. Toumanova, *Way of A Pilgrim*, 10.
9. Kadloubovsky and Palmer, *Philokalia*, 158–59n33.

mercy upon me!"—and force it, instead of all other thoughts, to have only this one constant cry within. If you continue to do this constantly, with your whole attention, then in time this will open for you the way to the heart which I have described. There can be no doubt about this, for we have proved it ourselves by experience.[10]

CONTEMPLATION AS LIFE IN GOD

Our discussions on the *prayer of the heart* and the *Jesus prayer* shed light on the nature of contemplation. The first thing we can say about contemplation is that it cannot be perceived as a mere act. Taken as a mere act to be performed, one can be deceived into thinking that if he or she performed the act of prayer correctly and with good intention, then his or her duty to God would be fulfilled. But if one's relationship with God does not lie solely in one's duty to God but on the desire for union with God and to live in that union, then one can't simply be satisfied by merely fulfilling one's duty; one must be united with God's Spirit as much as and as long as one possibly can.

When contemplation has been interpreted in the light of the *prayer of the heart*, the problem of *prayer as a mere duty* becomes evident. If one views prayer as a duty to fulfill, then prayer becomes one thing among others, a thing on the list of one's daily tasks. One prays to check off prayer from the list. This approach to prayer makes the activity mechanical and superficial. Not only does one treat prayer as a thing to do, to check off the list, one also tends to view God as an object among other objects to which one attends at the moment of prayer. This approach to prayer makes it difficult to imagine how the person relates to God outside of the allotted time for prayer. The truth, however, is that God is omnipresent. God does not make Himself present only when we pray. The key insight lies in how we recognize the presence of God in our life, and the *Jesus prayer*, as presented and discussed, aims to assist us in recognizing God's omnipresence by being in tune with God's Spirit in our own heart.

God exists as the Source and Ground of all things that exist. We cannot approach God in prayer as if God were an object of our attention only during an allotted time. If we do that, we turn God into an occasional object of our attention. In doing so, we limit God's presence under our limited condition to receive God's Spirit. What we should do in prayer is to *accept*

---

10. Kadloubovsky and Palmer, *Philokalia*, 33–34. (Note: We do not know the date of the birth of Saint Nicephorus. The short autobiographical note on Nicephorus indicates that he lived in the monastery on Mount Athos and died in 1340, see p. [x-ref]).

God as the Mystery of our life, not a mystery that awaits to be discovered by our own inadequate rationality and theological methods, but the Mystery that reveals itself to us in the silence of our heart. God is not an object of our study and research, though we may define, describe and construct meaningful statements about God to make some sense of the Mystery of God for ourselves and to communicate our findings to others. But in an ultimate sense, as the Spirit and Ground of all things that exist, God must be experienced personally in and through prayer. If we turn God into an object of study, our prayer will run the risk of being a mere exercise, and we can be inclined to measure the success of our prayer based on our reflection and analysis of our performance. Or we pray perhaps because we want an answer from God. God no longer exists as the Mystery of our life. We have projected our needs onto God, thus God becomes a God of our own creation. Contemplation is not and cannot be viewed in this way.

Listening to God's Spirit must be the first aim in contemplation. But how can we listen to God's Spirit in our heart if we approach God from the viewpoint of our own worthiness? We are not more or less before God's eye, because God creates us and knows us more intimately than we know ourselves. We are precious in God's eye and God loves us just as we are. To come to God in prayer with a self-worth attitude would be like the Pharisee in the Gospel according to Luke who prays, standing before God, saying, "God, I thank you that I am not like the other people: thieves, rogues, adulterers, or even like this tax-collector. I fast twice a week; I give a tenth of all my income" (Luke 18:11–12). The Pharisee is measuring himself up against the tax-collector, but he does so with his own sense of self-worth. In the conventional way of thinking in the society in which Jesus lived, a tax-collector was perceived by the public as a sinner. Whereas, the Pharisee was seen as someone who knew the law and the prophets; and thus he was considered "holy" by the standard observation and acceptance of the people in the given society. But the Pharisee's intention does not come from a humble heart but from his own self-worth. The tax-collector, in contrast, "was beating his breast and saying, "God, be merciful to me, a sinner!'" (Luke 18:13). The tax-collector stands before God as a sinner in need of God's mercy. He truly is praying the *Jesus prayer*.

In contemplation, we come listening to God's Spirit in our heart. But the Spirit with which we listen is a given, a gift from God. This means that the capacity for listening to God's Spirit is innate in us, but we have to listen to God's Spirit with the true self that God has created us, a self portrayed in a tax-collector from the Gospel of Luke. In the second story of creation in the book of Genesis we are told that God forms a shape of man from clay and he breathes his very breath into the man's nostrils to give him life

(Gen 2:7). This is a biblical way to describe the relationship between God and humanity. Every human person is created by the very breath of God for the purpose of having life with God forever. It also means that true life comes from God's Spirit, and it is from the depth of our spirit that we come to know God and our true self. In contemplation, we come to God with our true self, not the self that has been chocked off by the desire for material things and conventional ways of thinking, perceiving and acting.

No contemporary spiritual writer has articulated more profoundly the contrast between the *false self* and the *true self* in contemplation than Thomas Merton (1915–68), a Trappist monk of the last century. Merton keenly observes that the *false self* is the self that manifests in the world based on the measure of external reality. It is the self that gets its identity from external reality. In other words, the *false self* is measured by one's profession, state of life, social position, wealth and prestige. For Merton, this self is delusional because it tricks the person into thinking that his or her identity fundamentally depends on his or her external reality. The *true self*, in contrast, is the self before God, a sinner but loved and forgiven by God. It is this self that must be presented before God in prayer. Merton writes:

> Contemplation is not and cannot be a function of the external self. There is an irreducible opposition between the deep transcendent self that awakens only in contemplation, and the superficial, external self which we commonly identify with the first person singular. We must remember that this superficial "I" is not our real self. It is our "individuality" and our "empirical self" but it is not truly the hidden and mysterious person in whom we subsist before the eyes of God. The "I" that works in the world, thinks about itself, observes its own reactions and talks about itself is not the true "I" that has been united to God in Christ.[11]

At first glance, the passage seems to indicate the split between the physical realm and the spiritual realm and between the external self and the true self. But this seeming division will soon dissipate if we understand Merton's theological anthropology correctly. What Merton wants to assert is that contemplation is not and cannot be the function of an external self which we have mistakenly identified as our *true self*. The external self is the *false self*. It is the self that thinks, decides, and acts in the world. But the thoughts, decisions and actions of the *false self* are often conditioned by the conventional way of thinking, choosing and acting. The first step in contemplation is to be aware of this conventional self, and to let it be submerged,

---

11. Merton, *New Seeds of Contemplation*, 7.

so that the *true self*, one that is often hidden from us, can be awakened and emerged. The *true self* is the spiritual self, and it is the self that is revealed by God who is its Creator and Source. For this reason, for the *true self* to be awakened and emerged, it must be in tune with God's Spirit. But when the person comes to God with the *false self*, the channel between God and the *true self* is blocked, and thus, prayer becomes merely functional, and one is deceived in thinking that he or she has truly prayed.

IMAGE OF GOD IN CONTEMPLATION

Not only can our image of ourselves before God be delusional, our image of God can also be. In order to cultivate a healthy image of God one must, first, develop an awareness of the spiritual realm and cultivate a habit for thinking and perceiving a reality from a point of view of the spiritual realm. Many people, not aware of the reality of the spiritual realm and their need for an image of God that is transcendent and holy, project images of gods that are neither transcendent nor holy, but are mere higher powers. For example, material comfort, power and prestige can be projected and perceived as gods in this sense. Unfortunately, these are all human creations of gods rather than the transcendent being.

In order for the spiritual life to develop, one needs to cultivate the belief in a transcendental being whose existence transforms the physical world and whose power inspires him or her to imagine possibilities for communication to the higher being. In his book, *How to Know Higher Worlds*, Rudolf Steiner (1861–1925), a contemporary Austrian philosopher and clairvoyant, provides several crucial steps that help develop the soul's awareness of the spiritual realm and cultivate the spiritual self. Steiner describes spiritual experience as "feeling" and underscores the need to have a religious attitude about a higher being. He writes, "We will not find the inner strength to evolve to a higher level [of spiritual life] if we do not inwardly develop this profound *feeling* that there is something higher than ourselves" (emphasis added).[12] To attain this state of *feeling of the higher being*, Steiner insists that a *spiritual seeker*[13] must cultivate a certain fundamental attitude of the soul. This cultivation comprises three interrelated attitudes: 1) reverence for all existing things, especially human beings, 2) humility, and 3) the desire to use one's knowledge for the betterment of others. By *reverence*, Steiner means a sense of wonderment and respect for all things that exist,

---

12. Steiner, *Knowledge of Higher Worlds*, 17.

13. The term *spiritual seeker* is used in reference to someone who seeks for higher knowledge through intellectual and spiritual disciplines.

especially the respect for other human beings. This attitude arises in the person alongside the virtue of *humility* and grows in direct proportion to the latter. Steiner argues that any person who fails to cultivate humility will never be able to develop a sense of respect for other human beings and all existing things. The first step in attaining the state of humility is to refrain from making hasty and unnecessary judgments about other people. Steiner declares, "Just as surely as every feeling of devotion and reverence nurtures the soul's powers for higher knowledge, so every act of criticism and judgment drives these powers away."[14] Thus, a spiritual seeker must learn to see the good in everything, eliminate criticism, and withhold his or her negative judgments, not just on the surface in his or her behavior, but in his or her innermost thoughts as well. Finally, the spiritual seeker needs to comprehend and realize the truth that *one's spiritual knowledge is not meant for one's own enjoyment, but for the betterment of others and for the entire created reality*. Steiner writes, "Every insight that you seek only to enrich your own store of learning and to accumulate treasure for yourself alone leads you from your path, but every insight that you seek in order to become more mature on the path of the ennoblement of humanity and world evolution brings you one step forward."[15]

These three interrelated fundamental attitudes have already been embraced and practiced by many Christian contemplatives throughout the centuries. But the distinctive mark of the Christian understanding and practice of these attitudes can be perceived from the belief that the higher being no longer exists as a mere force, but has already manifested in a personal God, who though transcendent, has been revealed to humanity, first through the law and the prophets of the Old Testament, and then in Jesus Christ, the Incarnation of God, in the New Testament, as *the God of love*. In the Gospel according to Saint John, for example, Jesus says that he is *the way, the truth* and *the life*, and that no one can come to God the Father except through him (John 14:6).

Christian contemplation has, as its focal point, a union with the God who no longer remains aloof but in Jesus Christ has revealed God's self completely and irrevocably to humanity. In other words, Christians believe that in Jesus they find their *way* to God, and that way reveals the *truth* about God who is *life* eternal. To participate in God's life as it has been revealed in Jesus is the whole aim of Christian contemplation. Jesus is the mercy of God expressed in human flesh. When Christians contemplate the life of Jesus, they are moved by the way he relates to God and to other human beings.

---

14. Steiner, *Higher Worlds*, 18.
15. Steiner, *Higher Worlds*, 24–25.

They observe the way he prayed to God whom he called "Father" in times of difficulty and hardship and before he made an important decision. They learn from the way he taught his disciples how to pray. They are inspired by his acts of mercy towards the sick, the poor, the outcast and the neglected. They are moved by his compassion for the people who were hungry and thirsty and by how he fed them with his own words and the multiplication of the loaves and the fish. In all this, Christians experience a God in the flesh, and they unite with this God in their contemplation, so that they become what they contemplate. That is, they become united with Jesus' Spirit so that he truly becomes the *way*, the *truth* and the *life* for them right here and right now.

The intimacy between Jesus and God the Father inspires a kind of intimacy Christians want to cultivate for themselves in and through contemplation. Jesus calls God "father" and in the prayer "Our Father" he teaches his disciples to speak to God in the same way. So, the Christian God is revealed to us as a loving parent who created us for life forever with the fatherly God. But the image of God is not limited to "father." God can be a "mother" who reflects the motherly care for her children. This motherly image of God, too, can evoke in us a natural response to God as one of trust. Just as a mother or father loves his or her child and always wants the best for the child, so too God's love for us can be compared to a love of a parent for his for her child. But God's love is also more than any human love. We are fundamentally loved by God. This love can be experienced by the love of other human beings, most evidently through our own parents. But it also transforms any human love. Jesus says that there is no greater love than that of one who lays down his or her life for the beloved (John 15:13). He himself suffered and died out of love for God and for us. But Jesus's death was not the end of God's promise for us. God raised Jesus to eternal life. And so, in Jesus's resurrection, God's promise to us with eternal life has been fulfilled.

Christian contemplation is rooted in this belief, a belief that was, is and will remain as the Mystery beyond our grasp, for no one has ever seen Jesus's resurrection. The disciples of Jesus bore witness to his resurrection because he appeared to them after he had been raised; but they could not prove his resurrection. Despite this fact, they were moved to witness to his love to the world. The Mystery of Jesus's life, death and resurrection invites us to encounter God as the God of love, as the disciples of Jesus did. If we return for a moment to our discussion on Rudolf Steiner's view on the higher being, we can say that Steiner was correct in his observation that in order to cultivate the spiritual life, we must develop an attitude towards a higher being. But in Christian contemplative practice, this is one more essential step: the contemplative believes that the higher being has revealed itself in Jesus

Christ as a loving, personal and relatable God. Christian contemplation, at the foundational level, awakens the human heart to this fundamental truth about a higher being as the God of love.

THE REALITY OF SIN AS REVEALED IN CONTEMPLATION

Many Christians, however, do not, or rather cannot, experience the depth of God's love for them. There are several reasons for this. The most obvious reason has to do with the fact that, because of the demand of their life circumstances, many Christians have not taken the time to reflect on God's love for them. Another reason could be their not growing up in a religious household, thus not developing a habit of prayer suitable to experience the love of God in their lives. Also, how many who were brought up as Christians have let themselves be drawn into the current of the secular culture, in which the religious attitude towards a good and loving God is being shaken by the irreligious mentality. By this I mean that the Christian belief in a good and loving God is today challenged by the commonly acceptable scientific approach whereby empirical evidence is demanded for statements of faith, as in the old saying, "I'll believe when I see it." The scientific habit of thinking, which we are so accustomed to, and sometimes unconsciously operate on, has led us to doubt the existence of God because divine existence is not subject to observation and measurement. Faith in God cannot be scientifically proven. Rather, it is a gift given to us in the inmost depth of our spirit, as witnessed to by countless Christians throughout the centuries. We need to reflect on the love of God in our lives.

Christian mystics throughout the centuries have found an effective condition for recognizing God's personal love: the awareness of the existential reality of sin and the impact of sin. For Christians, God exists, not as a mere concept, but as a personal and relational God. Because of the personal and relational characteristic of God, sin is always relational. That is why sin cannot be perceived from a mere legalistic and/or moral point of view. From a legalistic point of view, sin can be compared to an "unlawful act." From a moral point of view, sin can be compared to an "immoral act." The Christian understanding of sin encompasses the legalistic and moral dimensions of sin, but it also goes beyond the legal and moral meanings and implications. Theologically conceived, sin is, first and foremost, an act against God, and by implication, it is an act against self and others. To understand the depth of the damage of sin, we must perceive sin from a divine-human relationship rather than as a mere breaking of a law or a moral conduct. It is true that every sin breaks God's law, for example, when one steals, he or she breaks one of the Ten Commandments; or when one bears false witness, he or she breaks another Commandment. But the consequence of an act of stealing or that of lying, reveals itself, first and foremost, as an act against God in that it damages the glory of God whose image is not reflected in the misuse of the human freedom to commit an act of stealing or lying. God's glory should have been reflected in the human freedom to choose the good, but in an act of sinning has now manifested itself in the brokenness of the human spirit as a consequence of sin. Second, by implication, the divine image with which the person is created, also becomes tainted by his or her sinful act; a person, in this case, becomes less of what he or she should be in terms of his or her own personal and spiritual development. Last but not least, every sin a person has committed is a sin against another or other persons in that a sin violates and even destroys the other person's dignity as creating in the image and likeness of God.

In our contemporary society, the consequences of sin have been diminished, and even done away with. There is a tendency to equate sin with guilt, and to seek help in dealing with guilt instead of sin. This confusion between sin and guilt leads to an illusion that just as guilt can be treated through psycho-analysis and be uprooted from the person's psyche, so it is with sin. When sin is being equated with guilt, then sin can be perceived and treated in the same way as guilt; that is, sin can be psychologized through psycho-analysis and be uprooted without a need for God. It is not surprising that so many have been led to believe, or rather, have been deceived to believe, that they have no sins after all.

Sin is a refusal to be good, holy and loving, essentially a refusal to become like God. To oppose the image of God with which one has been created is not natural to human beings, for we are not created to be evil. Being good by nature, God cannot create evil. The evilness with which we sin comes from another source than God. But what is that source if not nothingness? Evil comes from the refusal of goodness and manifests itself in lack of goodness. Sin is an evil act, an act from the lack of goodness. Sin, therefore, implies a contradiction, because sin resists the movement of God's creation in a person toward goodness. The consequence of sin, therefore, is suffering. Adam and Eve, our first parents, learned this lesson a hard way. The book of Genesis tells us that our first parents were living in an innocent state of life, a state where they only knew goodness. This was the natural state of life for them as God had intended. But after they had committed a sin of eating of the fruit from the tree of knowledge, their eyes were open and they began to experience suffering as a result.

Our situation today indicates to us that we are worse than our first parents; Adam and Eve recognized their sinful condition after they had committed the sin of disobedience to God. We, on the other hand, seem to have become numbed to our sins and their consequences. We have become more and more unaware of, or even indifferent to, the suffering we have caused to God in others and ourselves as a consequence of sin. As a result, we do not feel the need for God's forgiveness. This is unfortunate, because from a salvific point of view, there can be no salvation if there is no need to be saved. But aren't we all in need of God's salvation? We cannot deny the fact that hatred, injustice, intolerance, abuses and disordered and insatiable desires for material comfort, honor and fame have taken control over our life, both at a personal level and at a level of society as large. These realities are vivid manifestations of our sins. The reason we don't feel the need for God's mercy is that we haven't felt the impact of sin in our lives. But if we reflect for a moment on the damage sin has caused, we cannot but be stunned by the pervasiveness of sin in our lives.

As we reflect upon our current condition, the role of contemplation becomes evident. What contemplation can affect in us is that it can make us aware of the awfulness of sin, even though we may not completely understand sin. In contemplation, our sin becomes exposed. The horror of sin begins to reveal itself in the feeling of shame and confusion when we are confronted with two contrasting realities that have emerged in our consciousness: the love of God in bestowing on us the gift of free will to choose the good that lead to wholeness of life on the one hand, and our rejection of that gift in committing sin on the other hand. We realize that we can potentially obstruct the channel of God's grace by turning away from God, the Source of life, towards created things and to turn them into our idols. We experience, for the first time, that sin consists in how we may have, consciously or unconsciously, idolized created realities and chosen them over God. This awareness of the awfulness of sin stirs in us the need for repentance and the mercy of God.

PENTHOS IN CONTEMPLATION

In the history of Christian spiritual practice, there have been saints and mystics whose lives witness to the conversion from a sinful way of life to a life in search for God. The movement of desert monasticism in early Christianity, for example, became a spur to conversions. In the fourth century in Alexandria, Egypt, and in Constantinople, present-day Istanbul in Turkey, many early Christians decided to leave city life and fled into the deserts of

Egypt and Syria to live in contemplation. There are reasons for this. They were disappointed with the politics in the city regarding religious beliefs and practices. Disagreement about Christian doctrines among church and state authorities often led to the excommunication and exile of those who were considered heretical. Religious beliefs and practices often turned into political issues, and doctrinal decisions were often made by those who were in authority. Furthermore, material comfort and the desire for bodily pleasure had also proved insufficient for the human spirit. Thus many sincere Christians in the early Church fled to the desert where they dedicated their lives to seek God through contemplation. These desert monks were known for their long experience of seeking and finding God in the harsh conditions of the desert where they had to rely on God in their spiritual battle against the demons who many times tempted them to return to their former way of life in the city. The insights they gained as the result of the many years of spiritual practice proved helpful not only to their own spiritual life but also to the lives of many other Christians who came to seek spiritual guidance from them. For this reason, to this day they have been called "fathers" and "mothers" of the desert.

One important exercise commonly practiced among the desert monks is called *penthos*, a kind of constant sorrow and suffering as a result of one's own sin or that of another. Origen of Alexandria (185–254), one of the greatest theologians of the early Church, taught that each sin is like a wound; a wound can be healed over time, but the scar remains.[16] It is the scar that causes *penthos*. In this sense, *penthos* is a kind of a godly sorrow caused by the memory the wound of sin, which even after it has been healed, remains as a scar.

Among the early desert monks practicing *penthos*, one consistent advice they offered to those who sought their advice consisted in this: through contemplation God can reveal to the person his or her sinfulness, and as a result, the person mourns for his or her sins. Viewed from the divine-human relationship, *penthos is the work of God's grace; it does not come from mere human effort*, though the person who has received God's grace cannot but be moved to respond to God's grace in a holy sorrow. That is why *penthos* is often accompanied with tears. These are tears caused by the person's fear of the loss of his or her own well-being on the one hand, and the shame and confusion before the goodness and mercy of God on the other hand. The sadness ushers from God to the person, who in turn, acknowledges this feeling as a gift of grace, and is moved to return it to God in an expression of both sorrow and joy over the mercy of God. The recognition of sin, in

---

16. Feldmeier, *Christian Spirituality*, 100.

this case, opens up the possibility for God's redemptive work in the person, who otherwise would not have been able to feel the need for God's salvation.

The early Church's understanding of salvation highlights the existential reality of sin and the need for *penthos*. Salvation in this context not only pertains to heaven or hell in the afterlife, but also to the loss or gain of the person's wholeness of spiritual health in this present life. Those who practice *penthos* experience the effects of sin on the one hand and the mercy of God on the other, right here in this world. They know how their sins have damaged the image and likeness of God in which they have been created, and they feel deeply in their hearts the desire to return to the original image and likeness of God.

Viewed from this perspective, we see the difference between *penthos* and *self-pity*: *penthos* is not a self-centered or neurotic condition, though one subjectively experiences the sadness within one's heart. But the sadness one feels in *penthos* is directed towards God and towards one's self in God. *Self-pity*, on the other hand, focuses on one's own self-image and worth without a need to relate to God, the Creator and Source of that image. The distinction between *penthos* and *self-pity* is crucial in the spiritual life in that it helps the sinner realize the importance of God in his life, a realization that can only come as the result of the working of the Holy Spirit who inflames in his heart the memory of his sin and triggers the plea for God's mercy.[17] The sadness one feels, therefore, is always accompanied with gratitude; the two cannot exist without one another, as early Church scholar, Irénée Hausherr observes, "You cannot have *penthos* without *gratefulness*. *Penthos* without thanksgiving would be despair, sorrow that was not godly, while thanksgiving without repentance would be a presumptuous illusion.[18] In an ultimate sense, *penthos* is the mourning for the loss of the likeness of God in one's self and thus, one must be reminded by a permanent sorrow and God's mercy.

Stories of Sarah of the Desert and Mary of the Desert, among others, exemplify the ascetical practice of *penthos*. When they were young, both Sarah and Mary lived by giving in to the passion of lust. For many years they enjoyed pleasuring men, not necessarily for money, but for their own enjoyment. However, as they encountered the mercy of God, they were moved to change their lives for the better, often to the opposite extreme of their former way of life.

In the case of Saint Many of the Desert (344–421), for example, one day, on the Feast of the Veneration of the Cross, she decided to enter the Church of the Holy Sepulcher for the service; but she did not have the courage to

---

17. Downey, *New Dictionary*, 194.
18. Hausherr, *Penthos*, 19.

enter the Church because she felt overwhelmed by sins. At the same time, however, she was filled with contrition for her sins and so she prayed to Mary, the Mother of God, for help. The prayer triggered her conversion to a new way of life. The next day she returned to the Church and felt that she could enter the Church and attend the service. Her life, from that point on, changed from being a victim of lust to a penitent. Consequently, she decided to live as a monk in the desert, fasting, praying and mourning for the scar of her past sins; and she lived in this way until she died. For many years Mary cultivated the holy life through contemplation in the desert. Her experience of God's mercy strengthened her character as a sinner yet loved and forgiven by God. It was this bitter-sweet experience that moved Mary to dedicate her entire life to holiness and to assist others who came to her seeking for spiritual advice in their journey of return to God.[19]

DETACHMENT AND SACRIFICE IN CONTEMPLATION

There are many stories similar to that of Saint Mary of the Desert, the best known concerning Saint Antony of the Desert (251–356). Antony's parents died when he was about eighteen or twenty years old, leaving his younger sister and him orphaned. Luckily, Antony inherited the family's wealth. He was inspired by the word of Jesus in the Gospel according to Matthew, where Jesus says, "If you wish to be perfect, go, sell your possessions, and give the money to the poor, and you will have treasure in heave; then come, follow me" (Matt 19:21). Antony took Jesus' saying literally. He collected all the money he had inherited from the family's wealth, donated it to the poor, keeping a few things for his sister; and after entrusting his sister to the care of a respected convent, he dedicated his life as a monk in the desert of Egypt in search for God.[20] Similar to Saint Mary of the Desert, whose awareness of sins awakened her to the need for the Savior in whose mercy she had tasted, Saint Antony's conversion inspired him to the life of total dependence on God in the fight against temptations. Many times Antony was tempted by the devil who suggested that he should return to the former way of life with wealth and material comfort; but with God's grace he successfully resisted the temptations.

The stories of Antony and Mary of the Desert exemplify Christian holiness. The striking lesson we all can learn from them is that through the grace of God they came to know the difference between the two possible ways of life: one with wealth, bodily pleasure and material comfort but often

19. Feldmeier, *Christian Spirituality*, 98–99.
20. Gregg, *Life of Antony*, 31–32.

leads to destruction of spiritual well-being, and another renounces wealth and material comfort, to embrace a path that leads to fullness of spiritual life. The two paths of life presented to them a choice that was never easy. But they decided to choose the path that led to fullness of spiritual life, and they embraced detachment and sacrifice as a consequence.

Later centuries witnessed many other saints of the Church who also chose the path of life in ascetical practice. Saint Francis of Assisi (1181–1226), for example, came from a well-off family. His father was a prosperous silk merchant who wanted Francis to succeed him in his family's business. But against his father's wish, Francis dedicated his life to serving the poor, particularly the lepers. As a result, his father disowned him. Francis took Jesus's teaching on poverty seriously and he made it his personal call. One day, Francis decided to leave everything behind in order to follow Jesus. He stripped off his fancy clothes in exchange for a dark garment from a beggar which he wore girded with a cord, and set out to save souls. Francis eventually founded the Franciscan Order for both men and women who desired to embrace poverty as an ideal way of life in total dependence on God for the success of their ministry to the poor. Towards the end of his life, Francis was blessed with the stigmata, the impression of the five wounds of Christ crucified on his own body, signifying the spiritual grace he had received, a particular grace that enabled him to identify with the suffering of Christ in those who suffered.[21] Similar to Saint Antony of the Desert, Saint Francis of Assisi was aware of the temptation of the power of wealth and prestige and how the desire for material comfort could prevent him from the desire to serve Christ in the poor, the sick, and the neglected.

The story of Saint Ignatius of Loyola (1491–1556), a Spanish mystic and the Founder of the Jesuit Order, known as the Society of Jesus, exemplifies yet another pathway to holiness. Ignatius was an ordinary Christian who, in the course of his religious conversion, changed from a man dominated by the worldly desire for fame to the man whose desire was to serve God by doing God's will for him in the world. On May 21, 1521, during the battle against the French, who had claimed Pamplona, the territory in northern Spain, as their own, Ignatius decided to lead the Spanish troop on the front line fighting against the French. In an attack by the French army, a cannonball hit Ignatius's right leg, causing a severe injury. With their leader injured, his troop surrendered to the French army, and he was carried back to his family house of Loyola to be treated.

During the period of recovery, Ignatius was reading the *Vita Christi* (*The Life of Christ*) by Ludolph of Saxony, a fourteenth century Carthusian,

---

21. King, *Christian Mystics*, 73–74.

and the *Flos Sanctorum* (*The Lives of the Saints*) by Jacobus de Voragine, a thirteenth century Dominican. As he was reading these two books and reflecting on them, he experienced the two contrasting movements within his spirit. Ignatius later described the two movements in the following words:

> When he was thinking about those things of the world, he took much delight in them, but afterwards, when he was tired and put them aside, he found himself dry and dissatisfied. But when he thought of going to Jerusalem barefoot, and of eating nothing but plain vegetables and of practicing all the other rigors that he saw in the saints, not only was he consoled when he had these thoughts but even after putting them aside he remained satisfied and joyful (*Auto* 8).[22]

This experience happened to Ignatius almost any time he stopped reading and started reflecting on what he had read. He gradually became aware of two different spirits at work in him, attributing the cause of the feeling of dryness and discontentment to the evil spirit and to God the feeling of being consoled and content (*Auto* 8). He came to realize that *the things in which he took delight had no lasting value, while the response to Christ instilled in him a desire to know the Lord better* (*General Congregation* 35, Decree 2:4).[23] One observes that Ignatius became a new man whose passions for life remained the same, but the object of his passions changed from worldly ambitions to the greater glory of God, (or was at least the two were kept in tension). After his leg healed and he was able to walk again, Ignatius set out to search for God. He described himself as a "pilgrim" in search for the consolation of his wounded soul. Like the early desert monks and Saint Francis of Assisi, Ignatius was moved to serve God in serving others. He recorded the insights he had learned from God in his spiritual notes which later he composed into the Book of the steps of spiritual progress known as the *Spiritual Exercises*. The *Spiritual Exercises* of Saint Ignatius have benefited many souls throughout the centuries. They are a great resource and guide for Christians who search for God in their lives by doing God's will for them.

The stories of the conversions of the four Saints we have discussed: Mary of the Desert, Antony of the Desert, Francis of Assisi, and Ignatius of Loyola, share one thing in common: *Spiritual conversion is a work of God's*

---

22. Parmananda, *Pilgrim's Testament*, 9. (Note: In his *Autobiography*, Ignatius writes in the third person and refers to him as "he" and "him" rather than in the first person pronoun as "I" and "me." Thus, in the above cited text, the pronoun "he" refers to Ignatius himself. Thereafter, citations from Saint Ignatius' *Autobiography* will be taken from this translation, cited with *Auto* followed by the number of the paragraph.)

23. Padberg, *Jesuit Life & Mission Today*, 734.

grace in conjunction with human efforts cooperating together which enables human beings to turn away from sin toward God and to offer their lives to the service of God in serving others. At the foundation of every conversion experience lies the recognition of one's sinful tendency and the need to detach one's self from the things that can potentially lead to sin. In the case of Mary of the Desert, it was *lust*, a vice that expressed itself in disordered sexual desire that ultimately prevented her from experiencing God and her true self. For Saint Antony of the Desert, it was the temptation to return to the former way of life with *wealth and material comfort* after he had renounced them. Similar to Antony of the Desert, Francis of Assisi was also inspired by the desire for a radical poverty but saw *radical poverty* as the means for identifying with Jesus Christ in the poor and the suffering of the world. He was moved to serve them with love and compassion. Finally, Ignatius of Loyola experienced *vainglory* as the prominent vice that could potentially blind him in the search for God's will for him in the world. Ignatius was the man with talents and gifts, but before his conversion, Ignatius wanted to use the talents to magnify his own glory. His conversion, however, moved him to reverse this tendency by using the same gifts and talents in the service of God and others.

Three important points we can observe from the conversion stories of these four saints. First, detachment to created things has proved necessary in the spiritual life. Detachment does not imply that created things are somehow bad in and of themselves. The term should not give that false impression. However, the desire for wealth, material comfort, pleasure and self-enhancement, when it becomes disordered, can cloud one's judgments of created things; when created things are misjudged, they are inevitably misused; when they are misused, destruction often results. Thomas Merton offers insight into the need for detachment in the following words: "Everything you love for its own sake, outside of God alone, blinds your intellect and destroys your judgment of moral values. It vitiates your choice so that you cannot clearly distinguish good and evil and you do not truly know God's will."[24] Material comfort provides us with a sense of physical satisfaction. But when our desire for material things becomes disordered; that is, when we love material things without recognizing that they are God's gifts for our service of God, then we can misuse them for our own selfish purposes. Consequently, instead of a blessing they turn into a curse in our life. A self-centered spirituality always destroys us in the end.

Secondly, a continual practice of detachment often entails sacrifice in the letting go of the things that are not helpful to spiritual life. Jesus says in

---

24. Merton, *New Seeds of Contemplation*, 203.

the Gospel, "Unless a grain of wheat falls into the earth and dies, it remains just a single grain; but if it dies, it bears much fruit. Those who love their life lose it, and those who hate their life in this world will keep it for eternal life" (John 12:24–25). The word "life" in these verses contains a spiritual dimension. It does not merely refer to the afterlife as opposed to the present life on earth. Rather, it means "the wholeness of life" both now and in the afterlife. The true life is the spiritual life, one that manifests in this life that we have. But for the spiritual life to take root and flourish, certain aspects of the material life must die. Things belonging to the spiritual realm and things that belong to the material realm often oppose each other. It is not the material that gives meaning to life, but the spiritual. When material reality chokes off the soul's spirit, then life becomes a living death. Detachment and sacrifice are the two sides of the same reality of the spiritual life; without one or the other, the spiritual life cannot flourish.

Thirdly, detachment and self-sacrifice are not for their own sake but for the sake of the development of the spiritual life, with an aim to divine union. As we have observed in the lives of the above mentioned saints, the conversion from a former to a new way of life is attained through a vision enlightened by God's grace, one that enables the person to perceive the difference between the two ways of life: one leads to wholeness of life and another leads to destruction. Once the contrast between the two ways of life has been felt and appropriated, then the choice becomes evident: one must choose the path to wholeness of life. This insight offered by many mystics proves to be the most important spiritual lesson, especially for those who have advanced in their spiritual practice. These advanced practitioners know that mental disposition is much more difficult to attain than a physical one. Those who, by the grace of God, have been able to resist the temptations to wealth, material comfort and bodily pleasure, begin to experience a subtler kind of temptation: the attachment to one's own spiritual capability. At a higher level of spiritual awareness, one may feel inspired to choose material poverty as a way of life and succeed in doing so, but at the same time, he can be deceived into living a life of poverty for poverty's sake rather than for the sake of his spiritual growth. The same goes with regard to the desire for religious devotion. Devotion can be performed for the sake of performance rather than for the purpose of increased love for God. The inversion of the result can be reflected on and detected in one's spiritual movements when one senses that there doesn't seem to be a correlation between her pietistic acts and her own interior life. For example, fasting can turn into an ill-discipline of the body rather than for the sake of spiritual discipline; charitable works can turn into a mere performance for the sake of being seen by others rather than for the pure intention of helping others; and one's own conception of God can turn into an ideology rather than from an inspiration of grace.

These are but a few manifestations of a delusional form of detachment and sacrifice, and they are obscure and cunning and thus very difficult to discern. They tend to make their appearances like a good angel but they are in fact the worse obstacles to the spiritual life. To discern so as to deal effectively with these types of delusion, one must be aware of the direction in which his or her spirit is moving and to choose the direction that leads to God and goodness, not only to one's self, but more so to others, and to avoid the direction that leads to narcissism.

THE PURPOSE OF CONTEMPLATION

Christian contemplation has one and only purpose: *union with God*, which manifests itself in union of love. The word "love" used in this context connotes a deeper meaning than we ordinarily conceive of. It is rooted in the Greek word *agape*, which means "love for the sake of the beloved" or "selfless love." There are other manifestations of human love; for example, maternal and paternal love, love of friendship, romantic love. . . . *Agape* does not exclude these types of love, but it transforms them. In his first letter, Saint John addresses the early Christians in these words, "Beloved, we love because He has first loved us" (1 John 4:19). That is, we love because we first have experienced what it means to be loved by God. Authentic human love ought to imitate God's love, and the way we do so is through experiencing what it means to be loved by God, a love that comes through contemplation. God's love for us has manifested itself completely in Jesus' love. His was a selfless love (*agape*) for others, a self-emptying love that ultimately appeared as a sacrificing love in his suffering and death. Indeed, Jesus's love demonstrates the meaning of his teaching about love when he says, "No one has greater love than this, to lay down one's life for one's friends" (John 15:13). The end of Christian contemplation has nothing more than the attainment of this kind of love.

In our contemporary context, however, the word "love" is understood narrowly, and/or misused and abused. "Love," in our context, is commonly taken to refer to romantic love. We even use "love" to describe our attachment to and infatuation with certain things or people. This is why it has become difficult to make a shift in thinking and talking about Christian love in the way I have demonstrated. In a fundamental way, Christian love flows from God's love, because God is good and loving. The belief in a good and loving God who creates everything out of love, in particular, humanity with its capacity for self-transcendence in love, reveals to us that the purpose of contemplation is to awaken us to the depth of God's love for us, which in turn, enables us to embody God's love in the world. In this sense, contemplation awakens us to the religious truth that we are not self-made. God has made us, and God continues to create us through others. Everything we have received in our lives comes from the goodness of God, which manifests itself in the gifts, talents, generosity and goodness of ourselves as well as elsewhere including other people.

Furthermore, through contemplation we come to realize that the gifts we have received are meant to be shared. If the gifts are not shared, then we can be deceived into thinking that none of the things we have received are gifts from God and others, but are the fruits of our own efforts and success in life. Consequently, the gifts lose their spiritual meaning for us. We can be inclined to treat them in whichever way we want, including misusing and even abusing them for our own distorted purposes. In doing so, our lives cease to be gifts for others as God has intended, but become our own selfish creation.

In his book, *No Man Is an Island*, Thomas Merton eloquently captures one of the essential religious aspects of life by underscoring the truth that life is a gift from God and how that gift is meant to be shared. He does so from a personal reflection on his own religious experience of God, self, and others. Merton writes:

> My successes are not my own. The way to them was prepared by others. The fruit of my labors is not my own: for I am preparing the way for the achievements of another. Nor are my failures my own. They may spring from the failure of another, but they are also compensated for by another's achievement. Therefore, the meaning of my life is not to be looked for merely in the sum total of my own achievements. It is seen only in the complete integration of my achievements and failures with the achievements and failures of my own generation, and society, and time. It is seen, above all, in my integration in the mystery of Christ.[25]

Merton draws out the interdependence between the individual person's success and failure and that of other people and of the society as a whole. The individual person's perspective on the meaning and purpose of life in a given society intricately links to the meaning and purpose of life as they are understood and appropriated by the people in that given society. The trajectory of the person's life and that of the society as a whole are intimately interconnected. From the theological point of view, the trajectory

---

25. Merton, *No Man Is an Island*, xxi–xxii.

of human life depends ultimately on the inspiration and guidance of the Holy Spirit, the Spirit that has manifested in the Mystical Body of Christ which is the Church. It also means that God's ongoing act of creation of an individual person and that of the society as a whole is conditioned by the human recognition and acceptance of God's gifts and to cooperate with God's ongoing creation.

From the human developmental point of view, people have found that happiness often consists in the desire to give more than to receive. Narcissism is an enemy of human growth to maturity. Self-love is the greatest obstacle to spiritual growth. The narcissist tendency in spiritual practice has been observed by Rudolf Steiner as follows: "The purpose [of spiritual practice] is not to accumulate learning as our own private store of knowledge, but to place what we have learned in the service of the world."[26] Indeed, in Steiner's view, the person's spiritual development fundamentally depends on his or her ability to place his or her knowledge at the service of others. Steiner asserts further: "Every insight that you seek only to enrich your own store of learning and to accumulate treasure for yourself alone leads you from your path, but every insight that you seek in order to become more mature on the path of the ennoblement of humanity and world evolution brings you one step forward."[27]

Many mystics throughout the centuries have been made aware of the human tendency to misuse God's gifts. Ignatius of Loyola, for example, learns from his own experience that we human beings are essentially good and generous, but are also prone to selfishness and evil attempts. The reason for this is that our desire for self-love and pride can take priority over us and cloud our judgments of God's gifts. In the Principle and Foundation of the *Spiritual Exercises*, Ignatius clearly indicates that human beings are created to praise, reverence, and serve God, and by means of this to save their souls. For Ignatius, this is the purpose of human life. Other created things are meant to help human beings to attain their own salvation and to assist others in attaining their salvations (*SpEx* 23:2–3). This view implies that every person should have a healthy attitude towards created reality. This can be done by the person's attempt to maintain an attitude of being "indifferent" towards his or her gifts and talents, which does not imply that he or she should be "careless" or "unconcerned" about his or her gifts and talents; rather, it means that he or she should be free of any distorted views about

---

26. Steiner, *Higher Worlds*, 24.
27. Steiner, *Higher Worlds*, 24–25.

those talents and gifts and to use them for the purpose of God's glory and the flourishing the human life (*SpEx* 23:4–7).[28]

The love of God and the love of others are the two sides of the same reality in the Christian life. With or without the felt experience of its existential reality, the Christian doctrine can be grasped conceptually. But to the contemplative who has felt the divine union in her heart, the fruits of contemplation naturally and spontaneously move her to the love and service of others; whereas, a person who through her intellect can conceptually grasp the truth of this existential reality while may still not be moved to serve others.

The contemplative has experienced and come to realize that she is fundamentally loved by God in and through the love of others, and would be incomplete if she were to remain in and of herself. She understands that mysteriously she is connected to others and to all of God's creation, as one part relates to other parts and to the whole. Saint Paul makes this clear in his letter to the Romans: "We, who are many, are one body in Christ, and individually we are members one of another" (Rom 12:5). So she knows that her choices and acts affect others, and vice versa. She also knows that the sufferings of others are not just theirs, but mysteriously they are also hers. Again, Saint Paul observes: "If one member suffers, all suffer together with it; if one member is honored, all rejoice together with it" (1 Cor 12:26). In an ultimate sense, the divine love that she experiences in contemplation moves her to the depth of the Mystery of God's love for her personally and for the whole of creation. It is in this existential dimension of her faith in God, which she has experienced through contemplation, that she comes to realize the deep connection between the love of God and the love of others; they originate in the one divine love. She has appropriated this love and become its mediation in the world.

Not only does selfless love help explain the Mystery of God's love for us in Jesus Christ, but selfless love also satisfies the human desire for fulfillment. Seen from the psychological point of view, a person cannot achieve happiness just by becoming rich, famous and successful. If wealth, reputation and success were the true and ultimate measures of happiness, many

---

28. In the *Spiritual Exercises*, Ignatius presents the Principle and Foundation as the first consideration of the entire spiritual exercises. He first expounds the meaning and purpose of human life and the right use of God's gifts for the glory of God and the service of others. Central to Ignatius's insight in the Principle and Foundation is the concept of "indifferent." The concept should not be taken to mean "unconcerned," "careless," or "unimportant." Rather, "indifferent" means to maintain a state of balance in regard to created things, state of life and life circumstances, so that one can appropriate and rightly use them for the purpose of serving God in serving others. (References to the *Spiritual Exercises* will be cited as SpEx followed by a number of the paragraph).

rich, successful and famous people would have found their happiness. The fact of life, however, shows a contrary reality: wealth and reputation are not the true measures of the happy life. If one's life lacks emotional support from others and connection to the divine, his or her life becomes unfulfilled. Ultimately, it is the companionship with others, a companionship that is often found in the love and service of others, that gives meaning and purpose in one's life. Furthermore, the companionship that one shares with others is also often grounded in the belief in the divine transcendent whose existence inspires one to a life in selfless love. It is not surprising that many Christians through spiritual practice have grown more mature in their concerns for others. They have come to know that it is in the service of others that their lives become more meaningful and fulfilled.

There is an inherent relationship between Christian contemplation and the Christian understanding of the *faith that does justice.* The Christian view on justice has its foundation in the love of God in Jesus Christ. The saving power of God in Jesus manifests itself in his unconditional love for others. But this love is grounded in Jesus' intimate relationship with God. When we read about Jesus in the Gospel, we encounter him, first of all, in his union with God whom he called "Father." Jesus had an intimate relationship with God. In the midst of his active ministry, many times Jesus withdrew into solitude to pray and to grow into intimate relationship with God. It was the intimacy Jesus had with God that enabled him to love others as God had loved him.

Jesus' relationship with God, though cultivated in solitude, was never meant to be isolated. In his ministry, Jesus comforted the sorrowing, healed the sick, freed the oppressed and fed the hungry. In doing so, he reconciled the human family with God and with each other, because every healing act of Jesus carried with it the love, not only for those whom he had healed but also for those who had inflicted suffering on others. The most powerful act that manifested Jesus' love can be seen in his forgiveness of his offenders. Jesus forgave those who did him harm even as he was dying on the Cross: "Father, forgive them; for they do not know what they are doing" (Luke 23:34). One should not interpret Jesus' saying to mean that somehow Jesus did not condemn the evilness of his offenders' acts. Rather, Jesus' forgiveness demonstrates that only goodness can bring good from evil, and only justice can destroy injustice. If he returned to his offenders the same hatred and violence they had imposed on him, he could not have reconciled evil with good, injustice with justice.

Here lies the foundation on which the Christian view on justice rests: *justice does not mean fairness; rather, justice means right relationship with God, self and others.* We cannot love others as ourselves unless we have appropriated God's love for us in our lives. Similarly, we cannot treat others with justice unless we have appropriated how God has been just to us. No one among us can claim to be free of sin, but God has forgiven us first, and in forgiving us God has treated us, not with fairness, for a forgiving act of God does not base itself on fairness, but with God's unconditional love. God forgives our sin in order to bring us back to right relationship with God. Then, from that right relationship, we relate to others more justly; that is, we forgive them.

The indebtedness we feel is the indebtedness of a sinner before the mercy of God, and it is this indebtedness that triggers in us the empathy to treat others in the same way God has treated us in our iniquity. We come to realize that our service to others means that we must reconcile with them just as God has reconciled with us in forgiving us. This reconciliation is not based on whether or not other people have treated us with fairness; for at times, they do not, or rather cannot. But it is based on the gratuity we can offer to them precisely because they cannot provide for themselves. Reality teaches us that the conventional understanding of justice as fairness is not universally applicable. The reason is that we are not born into the world with the same capacity and opportunity. Some of us are fortunate to be born in a better condition of life than others, while others who may be born into poverty. Some are born into a loving family, while others may be orphaned, neglected and abused. In reality, the opportunity for flourishing is opened to some, while remaining closed to others. There is a sense that life is not fair, and so justice cannot be based on fairness. It must be based on compassion for those who are unfortunate. This sense of justice cannot be taught by mere doctrines and principles; it must be felt and appropriated through contemplation of the God who has incarnated in Jesus as it is recorded in the Gospels. When through contemplation, a Christian personally feels God's love for him, he can be moved to work for justice, helping to foster right relationship among human beings, as God has intended.

Chapter 2

Spiritual Discernment in the Contemplative Life

INTRODUCTION

THE LAST CHAPTER DISCUSSED the nature of Christian contemplation and the function of contemplation in the spiritual life. This chapter will discuss the relationship between spiritual discernment and the contemplative life. It raises the following questions: Since the contemplative life has as its ultimate goal the union with God, and union with God is grounded on the human experience of the divine, known as mystical experience, how then does one discern and assess mystical experience? What are the characteristics of a mystical experience? How does one discern the various spiritual movements from within his or her soul as a result of a mystical experience? What is the role of a spiritual guide in assisting a person in the discernment process?

In answering these questions, the chapter will begin by tracing the origin of the term "spiritual discernment" by exploring its usage in Scripture, particularly in the letters of Saint Paul. Grounding itself on the Scriptural understanding of spiritual discernment, the chapter will then explore how the early Church monastic tradition understood and practiced spiritual discernment. The last part of the chapter will present and explain some of the essential rules for spiritual discernment in conjunction with the discerning of God's will in the *Spiritual Exercises* of Saint Ignatius of Loyola (1491–1556), the Founder of the Society of Jesus.

SPIRITUAL DISCERNMENT IN SCRIPTURE

The English term "discernment of spirits" or "spiritual discernment" comes from the Greek term, *diakrisis pneumatōn*.[1] It was Paul who employed the term *diakrisis pneumatōn* in his first letter to the Corinthians. There Paul lists the various spiritual gifts: wisdom, knowledge, faith, healing, prophecy, *discernment of spirits*, gifts of tongue, and interpretation of tongues (1 Cor., 12:10).[2] What Paul insists upon in discussing these various gifts of the Holy Spirit is that all spiritual gifts, though different from each other, are from the same Spirit, and thus ought to be perceived as coming from the same divine source and for the same purpose, which is to guide the Church's members in their journey toward union with God and with one another.

Paul's understanding of spiritual gifts originates in his understanding of the Church as the Body of Christ. Paul's metaphor of the Church as the Body signifies the mystical truth about the Church. The Church originates with the Trinity as the community of love among the Three Persons of the One God: Father, Son and the Holy Spirit. In this sense, the Church exists from eternity with God. However, being love by nature, the Trinitarian God does not exist as a self-contained entity; rather God always desires to communicate God's love, which is God's very self, to humanity. That communication was initiated by God's election of Israel to be the people from whom Jesus, the Incarnation of God, would be born to the human family. The Incarnation of God in Jesus, therefore, is conceived as the focal point in the history of the communication between God and humanity. Jesus expresses God's love to humanity in an irreversible and irrevocable manner, so much so that in Jesus Christians have seen the total union between the divine and human spirits to a degree that no one has ever seen before or will ever see.

The Body of Jesus that died and was raised becomes the Mystical Body of the Christ of faith to those who believe that he is God in the flesh. Saint Paul's metaphor of the Church as the Body of Christ, therefore, has two interrelated dimensions: 1) the *divine dimension*, whereby the Church is seen to come from the divine source, and 2) the *human dimension*, a relationship among the members of the Church who are participating in divine life of God. In Greek philosophy, the relationship between the *body* and the *spirit* has been used to describe the relationship between the *visible* and the

1. Downey, *New Dictionary*, 276.
2. Emphasis added.

invisible: the body makes visible the spirit. The metaphor of the Church as the Body of Christ employs the same analogy: as body makes spirit visible, so too the Church makes visible the Spirit of Christ to the world.[3] In other words, members of the Church make use of their various gifts endowed by the Holy Spirit to the building of the Church in the world.

Members of the Church are "parts" of the Body of Christ by virtue of their Baptism and in the sharing of the same Body of Christ in the Eucharist. Each member of the Church depends on each other for the well-being of all, as Paul describes it: "For just as the body is one and has many members, and all members of the body, though many, are one body, so it is with Christ" (1 Cor 12:12). Christ, being the head of the Church, unifies all of his members into his one Body. Unity lies at the foundation of the Church, and all the gifts of the Holy Spirit are given to members of the Church for the sake of Its Unity.

Seen from this perspective, *spiritual discernment*, one of the gifts of the Holy Spirit, should not be taken separately from other gifts, but it should be conceived in relation to other gifts and together for the well-being of the Church as a whole. In other words, discernment of spirits depends on wisdom, understanding, prophecy, interpretation and other gifts of the Holy Spirit for its soundness and authenticity. Furthermore, discernment of spirits should not occur in isolation, for there is always a communal dimension in which the discernment process is carried out. Finally, since Christ is the head of the Church to which all members belong, it becomes apparent that the purpose of spiritual discernment is to assist an individual Christian, as well as the Christian community to which he or she belongs, to recognize the path that leads to union with Christ and with one another.

The need for spiritual discernment can be perceived from the root meaning of the word itself. To "discern" means to make distinction between one thing or person from another so as to recognize the thing or person that is being discerned for what it or he truly is.[4] In the context of the Christian life in Corinth, the *object of discernment* had to do with *the difference between true prophets and the false prophets*. Paul says that there have been false prophets who preach human wisdom, relying on human eloquence over and against Paul's proclamation of the wisdom of God revealed in the crucified and risen Christ. For Paul, the kind of preaching of the false prophets goes against everything he himself has understood about Jesus and the reason for his witness to Christ. The following words demonstrate the contrast Paul has drawn between the two kinds of preaching:

---

3. Rausch, *This is Our Faith*, 107–8.
4. Gallagher, *Discernment of Spirits*, 3.

> When I came to you, brothers and sisters, I did not come proclaiming the mystery of God to you in lofty words or wisdom. For I decided to know nothing among you except Jesus Christ, and him crucified. And I came to you in weakness and in fear and in much trembling. My speech and my proclamation were not with plausible words of wisdom, but with a demonstration of the Spirit and of power, so that your faith might rest not on human wisdom but on the power of God. (1 Cor 2:1–5)

Paul clearly grounds his preaching on the wisdom of Christ rather than on mere human wisdom. What helps him "discern" the difference between the two types of wisdom is the contrast of their results. For example, in discussing the fruits of the Spirit (*pneuma*), which are the results of the working of the Holy Spirit in the Christians, Paul lists them: love, joy, peace, patience, kindness, generosity, faithfulness, gentleness and self-control (Gal 5:22). This list of the various fruits of the Holy Spirit are, then, set in contrast to Paul's prior list of the fruits of the working of the flesh (*sárx*): fornication, impurity, licentiousness, idolatry, sorcery, enmities, strife, jealousy, anger, quarrels, dissensions, factions, envy, drunkenness, and carousing (Gal., 5:19–21).[5] So for Paul, *diakrisis pneumatōn* (discernment of spirits) is judging the difference between the two contrasting spirits, the working of the Holy Spirit and the working of the flesh. The latter has been under the influence of the evil spirit, whereas the former is guided by the Holy Spirit.

The New Testament gives us, besides Saint Paul whose spiritual discernment we have just discussed, Saint John, whose theology for the discernment of spirits derives from an incarnational theology. In his first letter, John places a strong emphasis on Jesus Christ, the Incarnation of God, as the object and ground on which the discernment of spirits rests. He writes, "Beloved, do not believe every spirit, but test the spirits to see whether they are from God; for many false prophets have gone out into the world. By this you know the Spirit of God: *every spirit that confesses that Jesus Christ has come in the flesh is from God, and every spirit that does not confess Jesus is not*

---

5. Paul uses the Greek word *sárx* to contrast with the word *pneuma* (spirit) to signify the two contrary spirits: one from the Holy Spirit which is also the Spirit of the Risen Christ and the other from the evil spirit. This connotation of *sárx* is not the same as the use of *sóma* (body). The body (*sóma*), being created by God as good, cannot be the source of evil. The flesh (*sárx*), on the other, when under the influence of the evil spirit, can oppose the Spirit of Christ living in the individual Christian. In the letter to the Romans Paul contrasts flesh to the Spirit as follows: "But you are not in the flesh (*sárx*); you are in the Spirit (*pneuma*), since the Spirit of God dwells in you. Anyone who does not have the Spirit of Christ does not belong to him. But if Christ is in you, though the body (*sóma*) is dead because of sin, the Spirit is life because of righteousness (Romans, 8:9–10).

from God" (1 John 4:1–3).[6] Like Saint Paul, Saint John points to the need to distinguish between true and false prophets in the discernment process. But he does so by underscoring the foundational belief in Jesus Christ as the ground and object on which the discernment should rest. The different contexts of the two Apostles and their different theological emphases called for different centers of gravity in discernment. However, for both Saint Paul and Saint John, Christ is the object and the ultimate reason for Christian discernment, though Paul explains his theology for spiritual discernment on the ground of spiritual gifts, whereas John directly relates to Christ as the object of discernment, and not to the obedience owed to God's commandments in the Old Testament.

In the Old Testament, particularly in the first Book of Kings, Solomon was asked by the Lord God, "What should I give you?" to which Solomon answered, "Give your servant an understanding mind to govern your people, able to discern between good and evil" (1 Kgs 3:9). Here the object of discernment is wisdom as opposed to ignorance, and the King's reason for asking for the discernment of spirits is based on the ability to govern the people to whom he has been entrusted by God. The implication is clear: in order to wisely govern the people of God, Solomon should choose between that which is good, not only for himself, but for the people, and avoid that which is evil. Thus, the whole purpose of spiritual discernment here, too, shares the similar theme reflected in the New Testament discussed above, namely, to discern means to differentiate between the two spirits, one from God the other from the evil spirit, and to choose that which belongs to God while to avoid the evil one. The theme of discernment of good and evil is also discussed in the Book of Deuteronomy as follows:

> I have set before you today life and prosperity, death and adversity. If you obey the commandments of the Lord your God that I am commanding you today, by loving the Lord your God, walking in his ways, and observing his commandments, decrees, and ordinances, then you shall live and become numerous, and the Lord your God will bless you in the land that you are entering to possess. (Deut 30:15–16)

The Israelites (the God's Chosen People) whom God addresses here through the mouth of the Prophet Moses, are told to choose life and prosperity over and against death and destruction. The criterion on which they ground the deliberation of their choices is to be the commandments of God which have been instructed by Moses. They are to observe the commandments of the Lord their God and to walk in his ways. If, however, they do

6. Emphasis added.

the opposite—that is, if they turn their hearts away from God and disobey the commandments—then they will perish (Deut 30:17). Thus, the reason for the discernment of spirits is grounded on the flourishing of life, and the objects of discernment are the commandments of God.

When we compare the discernment of spirits in the Old Testament, as just discussed, to that of the New Testament discussed in Saint Paul's letters and in the first letter of Saint John, we can observe a shift in perspective. *The objects of discernment in the Old Testament are the laws, whereas that of the New Testament is the teaching of Jesus Christ and his own person.* This shift in perspective from the Old to the New Testament in terms of the object of spiritual discernment does not imply that obeying God's commandments according to the Old Testament no longer has effects in the spiritual life. Rather, the New Testament shifts the object of discernment from observance of the law and the prophets to Jesus Christ, the Incarnation of God and Himself God, because Jesus has fulfilled the law and the prophets of the Old Testament in the way he loves God and others to the point of death on the cross. Jesus himself says, "Do not think that I have come to abolish the law or the prophets; I have come not to abolish but to fulfill" (Matthew, 5:17). Jesus's love for God and others led him to a humiliating death on the cross; but his life did not end there. Rather, God raised him up to life forever. Jesus's resurrection from the death is the promise of an everlasting life preserved for those who believe in him and want to live life in union with him. For this reason, Christian spiritual discernment has Christ as the focus. Christians strive to discern a path of life conducive to the following of Christ in the world and to do God's will, just as Jesus himself did, because in Jesus the wisdom of God has been revealed and fulfilled.

SPIRITUAL DISCERNMENT IN THE EARLY CHURCH

In the early Church, spiritual discernment, too, was grounded in Christ. In this regard, Origen of Alexandria (185–254) was arguably the most influential theologian. He invented the method for scriptural interpretation based on the three stages of spiritual development which he had adopted from Neo-Platonism. Origen attended the lectures given by the founder of Neo-Platonism, Ammonius Saccas (175–242).[7] Plotinus (204–70) was also a student of Ammonius Saccas. In his most famous work, *Enneads*, Plotinus collected the things he had learned from his master. The teaching most relevant concerning our present discussion on spiritual discernment is Plotinus's view on the relationship between the One and the Many. According

---

7. Rich, *Discernment in the Desert Fathers*, 13.

to Plotinus, there exists the One who is the source of all things that exist, and that everything that exists has a yearning for the return to their source which is the One. One must know that the term "One" employed by Plotinus does not represent the first number in a series of numbers. Rather, the One is the measure of all numbers and is itself not measured by anything.[8] Plotinus's employment of the One and the Many conveys his method for underscoring the dynamic relationship between unity and diversity. The One (unity) encompasses the Many (plurality). But the One, being a spiritual and transcendent Being, cannot manifest itself in the world except through the Many; whereas, the Many proceeds from the One and realizes its true identity when united with the One. The differentiation between the One (unity) and the Many (plurality) must be maintained for the union between the two to be possible. In other words, in the union between the One and the Many, the identity of the Many remains intact while it is transcended by the One. This means that in the state of union between the One and the Many, the diversity of the many things that exist are transcended by the One rather than being absorbed into the One.[9]

Pertaining to the spiritual life, Plotinus conceives the soul as the essence of the human being. However, while the soul is conjoined with the body in this world, it is necessary that the two co-exist in the person. The soul constitutes the essence of the human person, whereas the human body merely functions as the necessary means for the soul's spiritual practice in its journey back to union with the One. This distinction between the soul and the body lies at the foundation of Plotinus's view on the return of the soul to the One whereby the union between the two is achieved when the soul rises to the spiritual realm independent of the bodily senses and completely joins with the One who is pure Spirit.

The soul's return to the One calls for the spiritual progress in three stages. The first stage aims to separate the soul from the base reality of the world of bodily senses.[10] The essence of the soul belongs to the intelligible realm, but when conjoined with the body, the soul is affected by the condition of the bodily senses. For this reason, in its journey of the return to the One, the soul must separate itself from the bodily senses so that the soul's nature can be realized and fulfilled. It is not that the bodily senses are bad in and of themselves, but the knowledge gained by the senses is always conditioned by and limited to the realm of materiality, whereas the soul's pure knowledge rises to the spiritual realm and is able to contemplate the One.

8. O'Brien, *Essential Plotinus*, 18.
9. O'Brien, *Essential Plotinus*, 18.
10. O'Brien, *Essential Plotinus*, 21.

In order for the soul to rise and to function according to its pure nature, the soul must be purified from the stain of the base reality absorbed by the bodily senses. An analogy of a dusted window can be used to illustrate the point here. Just as it is difficult for a person to see an object outside the glass window when the glass is covered with dust, so too the soul's capacity for intellectual knowledge can be conditioned by the stain of the base reality that has been absorbed by the bodily senses. The soul needs to be purified of the stain of the senses in order to perceive reality with its intellectual capacity, just as the glass window needs to be cleansed from the dust to maximize its capacity for transparency.

The second stage of the soul's spiritual progress is attained by means of a higher degree of knowledge. After being purified from the stain of the base reality, the soul now can know the essence of the created world, not by logical reasoning, but through contemplation of the natural order of the created world. Plotinus believes that there is inherently an *essence in everything* that exists, and that this *essence* is recognized by the intelligent capability of the soul, when in its purity, the soul is capable of recognizing it. This understanding of the soul lies in the philosophical viewpoint which asserts that there is a *similitude* shared by the created order of things and the soul in that both the soul and the created order of things share in the Intelligibility of the One which is their source. The shared *similitude* functions as the "mediation" between the soul and the created reality which enables the soul to recognize the essence of the created order of things for what it truly is.

O'Brien explains the relationship between the first and second stages as follows: "The second stage completes the first and is never achieved without it. The first—propaideutic—is the *via negativa*, apophatic as the later mystical writers will say; it is the area of the rejection of images. The second, an interim stage, is, despite its purgative effects, positive and cataphatic."[11] In other words, in Plotinus's view the first stage is achieved by "rejecting" or "denying" the base reality of the world of the senses; whereas the second stage "affirms" the inherent goodness in the created order. As we can see, Plotinus does not completely reject the bodily senses; but he underscores the importance of the separation of the soul from the base reality of the senses.

The first two stages, once achieved, naturally lead to the third and final stage. But in the third stage, there is a shift in perspective in the understanding of the soul's knowledge. The first two stages succeed from one another, but they are only preparatory stages for the third stage. They are leading the soul *towards* union with the One rather than leading the soul *to* union with

---

11. O'Brien, *Essential Plotinus* 22.

the One.[12] In the third stage, however, the soul is journeying *to* the One by means of a mystical union. This kind of *knowledge by union* has been articulated in the Christian tradition as *apophatic* experience and is generally perceived from two perspectives.

One view describes the experience as the "dark cloud of unknowing," also commonly articulated as "knowledge of the unknown." Both descriptions signify the truth pertaining to the limitation of the soul's knowledge of God. The Intelligence of God, being that of the Creator, is uncreated, or unoriginated and thus, eternal. The intelligence of the human soul, in contrast, is the created intelligence and is confined within space and time. In other words, the essence of the soul is spiritual, but its spiritual capability is conditioned by the temporal; whereas, the Intelligence of God transcends space and time. This implies that the soul's mystical knowledge is *infused* by God rather than *gained* by the soul itself. Mystical theologians have described this kind of mystical knowledge as "knowledge of the unknown." This does not mean that God is "unknowable" to the human intellect, but that the knowledge of God is revealed rather than attained. The faculty of the intellect must be subsumed and eventually becomes passive, and when the intellect has become passive, then the soul is capable of knowing the divine, not by means of its own capability, but as revealed by the divine source. The origin of this view has been attributed to Gregory of Nyssa (335–95).[13]

The other view shared by Plotinus and Origen, influenced by Ammonius Saccas, declares that the capability to know the unknown belongs to the soul, but it is rarely operative.[14] According to this view, in the state of union with the One the natural faculty of the intellect becomes *enlightened* by the One, and thus it is capable of knowing the One by being united with It.

Both views shared one thing in common: mystical knowledge of the divine eliminates the duality between the soul and the One while they maintain their distinctive characteristics. The union between the soul and the One, when attained, satisfies the soul's yearning for the One, who is the source of the soul's desire and fulfilment.

As mentioned above, Origen invented the method for the interpretation of scripture in which three are three interrelated meanings of text: the *literal* meaning, the *ethical* meaning and the *theological* meaning. Furthermore, for Origen, Christ is the subject of all of the scriptures in that all of the scriptures point to him and find their fulfillment in him.

---

12. O'Brien, *Essential Plotinus* 22. (Emphasis added.)
13. See Feldmeier, *Christian Spirituality*, 84–86.
14. O'Brien, *Essential Plotinus*, 23.

It was Evagrius Ponticus (345–99), a learned monk of the desert of Egypt, who developed the three stages of spiritual progress from Plotinus and Origen. Deeply influenced by the mystical theology of Origen, particularly by Origen's three meanings of a scriptural text, Evagrius drew a parallel between Origen's scriptural meanings and Plotinus's three stages of spiritual progress, and he fused the two structures into one. As a result of this synthesis, Evagrius was able to develop a new structure for spiritual progress of the soul whereby each of the meanings of a scriptural text according to Origen corresponds to a particular stage of spiritual progress in Plotinus: the first stage corresponds to the *literal* meaning of scriptural text; the second stage corresponds to the *moral* meaning; and the third stage corresponds to the *theological* meaning. Similar to Plotinus who had conceived the final stage of spiritual progress to be the union of the soul to the One, Evagrius conceived the soul's journey towards union with God in a three-stage progress called *practical, natural,* and *theological*. The first stage aims to attain the soul's *apatheia* (or spiritual freedom from disordered tendencies towards the created reality) and to cultivate virtues. This stage results in the soul's *agape*, a capacity of the soul to love the created reality for what it truly is rather than loving it from the soul's disordered desire. The conversion from *apatheia* to *agape* comes as a natural outgrowth from the first to the second stage of spiritual progress. In the second stage, the soul recognizes the divine presence in the created world. The third stage signifies the final bliss of the soul whereby the soul is able to contemplate God as God is. In this final stage, *prayer is conceived a state of being* rather a state of acting. The three stages depend on each other in such a way that the lower stage gives rise to the higher stage, and the higher stage completes the lower one. *Apatheia* (spiritual freedom from disordered attachments) gives birth to *agape* (love), and love is the door to natural *knowledge* which leads to contemplation of God as the *final bliss*.[15]

In summary, spiritual discernment in the early Church cannot be seen apart from the overall goal of contemplation, which is the union of the human soul with God. But this overall goal of contemplation is conditioned by a more immediate goal known as *apatheia* and by the cultivation of virtues. It is only when the soul has been freed from its disordered attachments to the created reality and has developed the capacity to discipline the bodily senses that contemplation can be carried out and achieved. The method for the attainment of *apatheia* developed by Evagrius Ponticus, was reinterpreted

---

15. Feldmeier, *Christian Spirituality*, 107.

by John Cassian (360–435) after him, and has provided the foundation for later developments of Christian mystical theology.[16]

THE INTERACTION BETWEEN SPIRITUAL DISCERNMENT AND PSYCHOLOGY

The purpose of spiritual discernment, as we have discussed it, is to assist the contemplative (the one who prays) to discern his or her thoughts and thus to follow the direction in which the good thought is leading and to refuse the direction of a bad thought. This description of spiritual discernment is based on the understanding of the interaction between thought and desire and between desire and action. A thought can trigger a desire and vice versa, and a desire often moves to action. For this reason, in spiritual discernment, it is crucial to examine the origin of a thought and how a thought has moved. It is equally important to examine so as to be aware of how and when a thought has generated a desire, and how, sometimes, a desire gives rise to a thought. Christian mystics agree that the interaction between thought and desire is a real one; they also teach that this interaction often results in a particular choice we make and a course of action we carry out. Our thoughts and desires are intricately woven and they inform our choices and determine our actions. In his book, *Our Thoughts Determine our Lives*, the renowned Serbian mystic, Elder Thaddeus of Vitovnica (1914–2002), makes clear how much our thoughts influence the way we live. He writes:

> All that is good and also all that is not, everything comes from our thoughts. Our thoughts determine our whole life. If our thoughts are destructive, we will have no peace. If they are quiet, meek and simple, our life will be the same, and we will have peace within us. It will radiate from us and influence all beings around us—rational beings, animals, and even plants. Such is our "thought apparatus," which emits thoughts with which we influence all other beings. And everyone expects peace, consolation, love and respect from us.[17]

A few centuries earlier, Saint Ignatius of Loyola (1491–1556) reflected on the interaction between thought and spiritual movement in his *Spiritual Exercises*. In the description of *consolation* Ignatius observed, "Just as *consolation* is contrary to *desolation*, so the thoughts which arise from *consolation*

---

16. See Nguyen, *Apatheia in the Christian Tradition*, 8–29.
17. Smiljanic, *Our Thoughts Determine Our Lives*, 49–50.

are likewise contrary to those which spring from *desolation*" (SpEx 317).[18] Here Ignatius is describing consolation and desolation as spiritual movements of the desire of the will. He also underscores the fact that a spiritual movement (desire) can give rise to a thought. Ignatius's observation indicates a reversed order of direction in the interaction between thought and desire: instead of a thought giving rise to a desire, it is the desire of the will that gives rise to a thought. In spiritual direction, we are helped to see how intricate the relationship is between thinking and feeling, and how decisive both thinking and feeling can inform our choices and actions. An action follows a choice of the will, but if the choice is conditioned by the particular thought, then thought, desire and action are all interwoven and part of the puzzle in the discernment process. It is, therefore, equally important to examine the relationship between desire and action. A desire must be examined and clarified for its authenticity before a choice is made and an act is carried out. Perhaps that is why in an opening statement concerning the set of rules for the discernment of spirits, Ignatius indicates that the aim of the rules is to help the person to perceive (*sentir*) and then to know (*cognoscer*) the various motions in the soul, so that he or she can make (*hacer*) a good choice by accepting the good motions and rejecting the bad ones (SpEx 313).[19] The interaction between desire and understanding and between desire and action requires careful analysis of the movement of thoughts, and this is where the role of spiritual discernment becomes crucial in the spiritual life.

The interaction among desire, thought, choice and action is indeed complex, and thus to discern their authenticity one must know the psychological dimension that operates in one's own thinking, desiring, choosing and acting. The question should now be raised: what is the relationship between spiritual discernment and psychology? The reason for raising the question here in our discussion is because of common mistake people often make in attributing characteristics of spiritual discernment to psychoanalysis and vice versa. In spiritual discernment, the reason behind the need to detect good and bad thoughts and to discern them should not be found on a mere psychological ground whereby the main concern is to conduct a

---

18. Ganss, *Spiritual Exercises* of Saint Ignatius of Loyola, 25–26 (italics are mine). Hereafter, citations from the *Spiritual Exercises* of Saint Ignatius will be taken from this translation and cited as "SpEx" followed a paragraph number. (Note: The *Spiritual Exercises* of Saint Ignatius is often given in the context of a retreat. In that context, the one who gives the Exercises is often referred to as the "director" and the one who receives the Exercises is often called the "retreatant").

19. Reference to Spanish words comes from the original text of the *Spiritual Exercises* of Saint Ignatius.

scientific study on the interaction between mind and human behavior. A Christian doesn't spend time and energy on conducting spiritual discernment merely on the need for processing his or her thoughts and feelings in order to know their causes and to treat them according to psychological and neurotic understandings of the human psyche. If that were the case, spiritual discernment and psychology would be conflated and there would be no need to distinguish between the two disciplines.

In insisting on the difference between spiritual discernment and psychology we are not saying that they are not interrelated, for it is true that psychological and neurotic knowledge of human thoughts and feelings and how the latter impact our behaviors and overall health plays an important role in the spiritual life. It is also true that oftentimes psychological knowledge provides important insights into how the human psyche works and thus helps us better understand how psychological and neurotic conditions impact human spiritual development.

Furthermore, spiritual discernment functions as an effective tool in assessing religious experience, for oftentimes amid spiritual movements, the psychological dimension of human development needs to be taken into consideration in the discernment process. Many psychologists have argued that religious experiences are psychologically constructed and that they exist as a mere result of an interaction between social constructs and the human psychological interpretations and reactions to these constructs.[20] The argument is plausible, since religious experiences are indeed "human" experiences and thus ought to be assessed through human rationality. But the argument does not do justice to the religious dimension of the divine experience; namely, that while constructed by human psychological process, the experience has been inspired and revealed by God's grace. From the theological perspective, grace has the capacity to transcend human rational capability, so when assessing a religious experience, that is, when processing and discerning the spiritual movement from within, the transcendental dimension of the experience becomes crucial. Most Christian mystics share the view that religious experiences are mediated primarily by religious affections and that they have God as the primary content and orientation.[21]

The relationship between psychology and spiritual discernment has been further explained by Michael O'Sullivan in his article entitled, *Trust Your Feeling, but Use Your Head*. In it O'Sullivan discussed the relationship between feeling and reason in the discernment process in the *Spiritual Exercises* of Saint Ignatius of Loyola. He asserts that emotions and cognitions

---

20. Hay, "Experience," 426–27.
21. See Saliers, *Soul in Paraphrase*, 6.

are highly interactive and interdependent; he also places an emphasis on the use of reason in the discernment process.[22] According to O'Sullivan, in discerning God's will, which is an object of Ignatian spirituality, one might make a mistake by using the religious experience as the principal criterion. One is attributing the cause of the spiritual movement to God while in fact, what is going on may have been the result of the interaction between one's emotions and cognitions that have nothing to do with God. O'Sullivan calls this a "mistake in the attribution process."[23] One attributes the characteristics of human experience to divine experience without proper attributions of correlated elements.

O'Sullivan's psychological insight proves helpful to our discussion. It points to the fact that religious experiences and the decisions one makes based on them have psychic dimensions. He underscores the interaction between thoughts and feelings, and he cautions us to be rational about the discernment process by not confusing mere human feelings with religious affections for God. His argument, therefore, ought to be taken seriously in conducting spiritual discernment.

But the point I want to make here is that *there is a difference in the way a psychologist arrives at his or her decision from that of a spiritual theologian.* This difference lies in the method each employs and the conviction each has in regard to religious experience. Psychology is an empirical science. Its method is based on empirical data and logical reasoning. Such a method, in theory, need not have God as its content. Similar to psychology, spirituality is a study of human life force and how to balance and direct that life force to human flourishing rather than destruction. But unlike psychologists, spiritual theologians approach spiritual discernment from the belief that God interacts with the world through human choices and actions. Human choices and actions, therefore, ought to be discerned and carried out under the guidance of God's Spirit.

Seen from this perspective, spiritual discernment aims to assist the person in his or her contemplation so as to grow in their relationship with God, self and others. In Christian discernment, the object of the discernment is God and the direction of one's life in God. Spiritual discernment presupposes this fundamental belief. A Christian may make use of psychological knowledge (and other human knowledge) only to the extent that they help them to further their progress toward spiritual discernment and growth. Beyond that, human knowledge should yield the spiritual discernment process whereby one's faith in God must be the guiding light.

22. O'Sullivan, "Trust Your Feeling, but Use Your Head," 17.
23. O'Sullivan, "Trust Your Feeling, but Use Your Head," 24.

The work of the evil spirit from within one's soul must now be discussed and explained. In the Christian tradition, it is agreed that struggle must be the first step in the spiritual life. The person who discerns the various spiritual movements, therefore, must wrestle with the force of the evil spirit which seeks to obstruct and destroy his or her desire for union with God. Hence, spiritual discernment, at the most fundamental level, implies the desire to choose a path that's guided by the Holy Spirit and to refuse the path that's influenced by the evil spirit. From this point of view, the chief discerner, therefore, is neither one's own self, nor is it the spiritual director to whom one turns for spiritual guide, but the Holy Spirit. It is fundamentally the battle between God who seeks to give life and the evil spirit that seeks to destroy life. Human beings are caught in between the two forces; they must choose the path that leads to God and life. Not only does one discern in order to choose God, but one's desire to discern itself manifests God's initiation and involvement in human life. God, therefore, is the chief discerner in the process; human beings are the actual discerners who discern under the guidance of God's Spirit. This is the pivotal point, one that cannot be overlooked in spiritual discernment. Many Christians, including those who are advanced in spiritual discernment, can sometimes makes serious mistakes when they do not follow this most important practice.

THE ROLE OF SPIRITUAL DIRECTOR IN SPIRITUAL DISCERNMENT

Spiritual progress needs discipline, and the cultivation of spiritual discipline is an art that can and should be learned. In the Christian tradition, since the early centuries of the Church, the guidance of an experienced spiritual guide has been understood as the necessary element in the practice of spiritual discernment. In desert monasticism, for example, it was a common practice among the monks to seek spiritual advice from each other, especially from the most experienced practitioner. There are two reasons for this. *First, there is a danger in relying on one's own spiritual movements and to discern them without knowing which movement leads to God and life and which movement leads to evil and destruction.* The discernment process requires the person who searches for spiritual guidance to talk to his or her spiritual director, who is willing and capable of listening to one's spiritual movements and to offer spiritual advice.

This important practice in the spiritual life has been insisted on by the desert monastic spiritual fathers and mothers. For example, many came to the desert of Egypt to seek spiritual advice from Saint Anthony of the desert

(251–356), because Saint Anthony was known for his spiritual insights and the ability to detect the spiritual movements in another person with quickness and precision. Subsequent development of monasticism never departs from this most central practice. John Cassian (360–435), for example, insisted that a monk should embrace humility by revealing his or her spiritual movements to the elders in the community. It is without a doubt that opening one's heart to another person to reveal one's spiritual movements and to ask for advice indeed requires humility on one's own part and trust in the spiritual director. Cassian teaches the monks in his community to embrace humility in spiritual discernment because only humility can counter the prideful tendency of one relying on one's own spiritual discernment without feeling the need to seek advice from another who is more experienced. The humble spirit enables one to listen more attentively to his or her own spiritual movements so as to judge their authenticity.

No one who has grown in the spiritual life will deny that humility is the most crucial virtue in the spiritual life. But the concept of humility in spiritual life needs further explanation. We are accustomed to perceive humility in relationship to others, particularly a humility enforced in one's own shortcomings and incapability to achieve what others can. In this sense, humility is perceived in terms of being in lower status than others. This understanding of humility reflects only one side of the kind of humility needed in spiritual progress. In the spiritual life, humility is a felt experience before the mercy of God. It is a kind of humility that can only be felt when one has come to recognize one's own sinful tendency then, in the face of one's own sinfulness, accepts God's love and mercy. In this sense, humility is not just a virtue; rather, it is the condition for the realization of one's identity in God.

Personal sin has a history, and in spiritual discernment one is encouraged to discern his or her history of sin. This history of personal sins over time comprises what is often described as the "core sin." One's core sin often does not exist as an actual sin, but it lies hidden at the root of the sins that one is prone to commit. The "core sin" develops differently from person to person. For some, the sin manifests itself in lust; for another, greed; for another, pride; and for another, anger, or one of the other vices. Whatever this core sin may be, one knows it by being aware of one's struggle against it, and if one has been struggling against one's "core sin," one is already a step forward in the spiritual life. The problem occurs when one is either unaware of one's "core sin"; or he may be aware of it but does not fully understand the damage it causes in his or her life and in the lives of others. In short, "core sin" can blind the person from recognizing a path of life that leads to flourishing and thus from choosing it. The force behind this blindness is pride. Spiritual pride is a clear sign of the influence of the evil spirit. Only humility can counter spiritual pride. That is why in spiritual discernment one is strongly encouraged to seek advice from a spiritual director. Self-reliance in spiritual discernment often creates problems in the end. John Cassian observes, "The Devil drags a monk headlong to death by way of no other sin than that of submission to private judgment and neglect of the advice of our elders."(*Conference* 2:11, 10).[24]

There is a caution also for the spiritual director. *The spiritual director should not think of himself or herself as a chief discerner and act as if truly being one.* The chief director in the spiritual discernment process is the Holy Spirit who alone can ultimately know the human heart and can guide that heart in the right direction. This factor in spiritual discernment can be either overlooked or misinterpreted by the spiritual director, particularly in the case when he or she becomes so closely involved in the spiritual movements of the one who comes for advice. For insight in this regard, we turn to Saint Ignatius of Loyola. In one of his preparatory notes in the *Spiritual Exercises*, Ignatius instructs the director in the following words:

> The one giving the *Exercises* should not urge the one receiving them toward poverty or any other promise more than toward their opposites, or to one state or manner of living more than to another. Outside the *Exercises* it is lawful and meritorious for us to counsel those who are probably suitable for it to choose continence, virginity, religious life, and all forms of evangelical perfection. But during these *Spiritual Exercises* when a person is seeking God's will, it is more appropriate and far better that the Creator and Lord himself should communicate himself to the devout soul, embracing it in love and praise, and disposing it for the way which will enable the soul to serve him better in the future. Accordingly, the one giving the *Exercises* ought not to lean or incline in either direction but rather, while standing by like the pointer of a scale in equilibrium, to allow the Creator to deal immediately with the creature and the creature with its Creator and Lord. (SpEx 15)

Maintaining an attitude of "standing by like the pointer of a scale in equilibrium" allows the director to be as objective as possible about to the spiritual movements of the retreatant[25], and thus to advise the retreatant based on careful and objective observation of the retreatant's interior movements. In other words, the director's task is to listen attentively to the

---

24. Luibheid, *John Cassian: Conferences*, 72.

25. The term "retreatant" refers to a person who is making the *Spiritual Exercises* of Saint Ignatius under the guidance of a spiritual director.

retreatant and to identify the direction of the retreatant's spiritual movements without feeling the need to make a decision for him or her. In this way, while maintaining his or her independence from the director, the retreatant benefits from the director's suggestions to discern his or her own spiritual movements with the guidance of the Holy Spirit.

Because of his own experience of God, Ignatius, like many mystics in the Christian tradition, came to believe that *God communicates directly to the human soul*, and that the human soul in contemplation, when has been purified from disordered attachments, is able to receive God's Spirit from within. Karl Rahner (1904–84), a Jesuit theologian, describes this kind of human experience of God as a "mediated immediacy." For Rahner, this term does not imply a contradiction. To say that God's presence is "immediate" does not imply that it is unmediated; for every experience of God, being a human experience of the divine, must be mediated through the human faculty of senses and intellect. But Rahner insists on the "immediacy" characteristic of the experience of God so as to underscore the characteristic of God's presence as "direct," rather than drawn from a dogmatic statement or derived from logical reasoning. In other words, the experience of God is directly given. To speak of its "immediacy" is to state God's desire to communicate to the person God's love, which is unique, personal and direct. But precisely because of its unique and personal characteristic that the experience is always mediated through the person's concrete reality. In this sense, the experience can be conditioned by the person's context and the degree of his or her disposition to God's grace. But in the case of a "direct" experience of God, the soul is most open to receive God's grace, and so God is able to communicate with the soul more directly than in other times when the soul is not disposed to the communication of God to the same degree.[26] The spiritual director's task in this case is to listen to the person's spiritual movements and to help affirm the characteristic of the experience as one coming from God.

SPIRITUAL DISCERNMENT IN THE SPIRITUAL EXERCISES OF SAINT IGNATIUS

I have already discussed some of the rules for the discernment of spirits in the *Spiritual Exercises* of Saint Ignatius thus far in this chapter, but I have not done so thoroughly. For the rest of this chapter, therefore I intend to focus on the particularity of Ignatian Discernment, which is the discernment of God's will for the individual Christian. In this regard, the *Spiritual Exercises*

26. See Rahner, "Experience of Self and Experience of God," 83, 123.

of Saint Ignatius provide a most complete and relevant method for spiritual discernment in our contemporary context.

The *Spiritual Exercises* of Saint Ignatius, just as any other spiritual practices in the early tradition of the Church, aims to help the contemplative achieve union with God. But Ignatius differs from the early traditions in that he conceives this union as the union of the human will to the will of God. Concretely speaking, Ignatius believes that God's act of creation of the individual human person is an ongoing act, which requires the person's cooperation through discovering of God's individual will for him, to be carried out in the world through his choices and acts. To speak in a more personal term, each individual Christian can say that by virtue of baptism, I am called to holiness. This is a calling to discover God's will for me. In discovering God's will for me, I come to realize how God is creating me through my choices and acts. At the same time, I also come to realize that the desires of my will are not always in tune with God's desires for me. Rather, they can become "disordered," and when they are, they obstruct God's desires for me, so that I cannot know God's will for me in the world.

The *Spiritual Exercises* of Ignatius are structured in such a way that if a retreatant makes the whole *Exercises* under the guidance of a spiritual director, he or she will more likely recognize the pattern of disordered desires and will want to uproot them so as to readily discover the will of God. Ignatius clearly states the twofold purpose of the *Spiritual Exercises* as follows, "[The *Spiritual Exercises*] aim to rid the soul of all its disordered affections and then, after their removal, to seek and find God's will in the ordering of our life for the salvation of our soul" (SpEx 1).

The term "disordered affections" deserves some explanations. To assert that there are "disordered" affections of the will implies that there are "ordered" affections. The distinction between the two types of affections is crucial in understanding Ignatian spirituality. Ignatius does not teach that one should get rid of all of his or her desires. In fact, the *Spiritual Exercises* has one ultimate aim: *to transform and redirect human desires for worldly ambition into the desires for God*. It would be a mistake to think that the *Spiritual Exercises* aim to help a person to suppress or remove all of his or her desires.

To further explore what Ignatius means by "disordered affections," and how one may recognize disordered affections in one's life, let us compare "disordered affection" to "addiction." By definition, an addict is someone who has lost control over his or her own judgments. His or her judgments are conditioned by an imbalanced distribution of the chemical substance in the brain, and thus they do not correlate to reality. In his book, *Addiction and Grace*, Gerald May, a psychiatrist and spiritual counselor, reflects on the nature of addiction and tells how addiction obstructs the channel of God's grace in the addict. "Addiction," he observes, "exists wherever persons are internally compelled to give energy to things that are not their true desires. To define it directly, addiction is a *state* of compulsion, obsession, or preoccupation that enslaves a person's will and desire."[27] In theological terms, addiction is a form of "disordered attachments" that needs to be removed before the person can be free to make choices that are authentic to his desire, which is also God's desire for him.

Ignatian spiritual discernment serves as an effective tool to help the retreatant realize his or her disordered affections and to object them to the love of God. The human intellect understands the damage of sin by contrasting it to the beauty and goodness of God's love. It is only then that the sinful person can turn away from his or her sinful pattern of life and turn toward God. Thus, we can see that the first step in countering a disordered affection is to recognize God's personal love. From the theological perspective, the removal of disordered affections does not at all imply the removal of all affections. The aim is to transform disordered affections into authentic desires and redirect them to love of God, who in his infinite mercy has created me for love. The concept of "detachment" in the spiritual life can now be properly understood, as Gerald May observes, "An authentic understanding of detachment devalues neither desire nor the objects of desire. Instead, it aims at correcting one's relationship to God."[28] In other words, a disordered affection can be compared to a "core sin" discussed above in that it is not a sinful act but exists as a desire that has been disordered, so that it becomes the cause of all sins. The only way to remove this disordered desire is to object it to the love of God in whose grace the disordered desire can be transformed and redirected to God.

In an Ignatian retreat, it is crucial that a person who has struggled with an addictive impulse, meditate on the profound sense of God's love for her. An addict can feel powerless before that condition and be afflicted with low self-esteem and a sense of unworthiness. Thus, the person can raise questions indicating confusion and doubt about their own purpose in life. It is here that the story of Ignatius's own conversion can provide us with a point of reference.

Ignatius had his own concept of disordered desire although he did not describe and explain it in the way we do with the term "addiction." Nonetheless, Ignatius's disordered symptom shares similar characteristics of an addiction. For example, Ignatius himself struggled with his disordered

27. May, *Addiction and Grace*, 14.
28. May, *Addiction and Grace*, 15.

tendency to self-love and pride. He knew by his own experience how the desire for self-love and pride, which in his case, often manifested in the longing for praises from other people, could blind his own judgments about who he was and what he truly wanted. Ignatius reflected in his *Autobiography* that as he was reading about the lives of the saints and the life of Jesus Christ, his mind was raised to a different level of understanding of his desires. He began to recognize, for the first time, a different kind of spiritual movement in him, one that was more quiet, peaceful and life-affirming, that moved him to the desire to serve God and others. Then he contrasted this new spiritual movement with the one he used to experience, one that would excite him first but gradually left him with dryness and distaste for life because it was the desire originating in his egoistic self (Auto 8). This was the first lesson Ignatius learned in the spiritual life that *in order to turn away from a destructive pattern of life, one must know another alternative that is better and life-giving, and that only God's grace, manifested as love, can enlighten the human mind to recognize his or her disordered affections and to turn away from them.*

In our days, disordered affections manifest themselves in various forms of addiction; for example, substance abuse, eating disorder, compulsive buying, and excessive use of electronic devices. These are patterns of life that obstruct God's grace from affecting us to desire for wholeness and authentic self. The *Spiritual Exercises* of Saint Ignatius, as a spiritual tool, can help reorient and redirect these disordered desires to holy and authentic desires.

The *Spiritual Exercises* of Saint Ignatius is structured in a four-week format. In the first week, Ignatius, in various exercises on sin, has the retreatant considering the sin of angels, and then mediate on the sin of Adam and Eve (SpEx 50–51). In these exercises, Ignatius encourages the retreatant to use his or her memory, imagination and reason to understand the damage sin has done to human beings, and how offensive sin has become to God. In doing so, Ignatius stirs a sense of shame and confusion in the retreatant who is confronting the reality of sin before the good and loving God. Ignatius writes, "In the present meditation [on sin], it [the object of my desire] will be to ask for shame and confusion about myself, when I see how many people have been dammed for committing a single mortal sin, and how many times I have deserved eternal damnation for my many sins" (SpEx 48). Then, Ignatius leads the retreatant to the contemplation on his or her own sins. Here Ignatius recommends that the retreatant should ask for the grace to feel an intense sorrow and tears for one's sins (SpEx 55). Then, by activating the faculties of memory, imagination and reason, the person recalls his sins and to consider how damaging and destructive they have become in his life. The point, however, is not to dwell on the ugliness of sins, but to come out of that condition by acknowledging and accepting the truth that despite their being sinful, God loves them and wants them to turn away from a sinful way of life toward God.

In the second week of the *Spiritual Exercises*, Ignatius helps the retreatant to envision Jesus as the Eternal King who calls her to a new way of life. Ignatius does so by presenting a series of exercises to describe and explain the vision of Jesus Christ for humanity. This vision of Christ originates in Ignatius's conversion at Loyola. We recall that during his time of convalescence at Loyola, Ignatius daydreamed about exploits he would do to impress noble women. But also he was reading and reflecting on the *Vita Christi* (The Life of Christ) and the *Flos Sanctorum* (The Lives of the Saints). Upon reflecting on his reactions to what he read, Ignatius came to be aware of two different spirits working in him: one stirred in him a feeling of joy and contentment as he dreamed about doing great things for Christ, and the other would excite him initially but afterward would sadden him as he was thinking about the heroic deeds of his past life (Auto 8). Peter-Hans Kolvenbach, the Superior General of the Society of Jesus from 1983–2008, observes that since his conversion at Loyola, Ignatius already centered his life on the service of Christ the King. Christ became the point of reference regarding his desires, choices and actions. Kolvenbach writes, "It is precisely in the experience of meaninglessness, of disgust with life, and of the joy of living to serve Jesus that [Ignatius's] encounter with Christ occurs."[29]

By the end of the first week of the *Spiritual Exercises*, it becomes clear to the retreatant that he or she has experienced the mercy of God. But the experience does not remain static; rather it turns into a dynamic that moves the retreatant to do something about his or her life, namely, to make choices in following Jesus Christ in the world so as to counter any tendency toward choices that lead to destruction. The *Call of Christ the King* further deepens the retreatant's desires of repentance by transforming them into the desire to serve Christ in his mission. Ignatius invites the retreatant to imagine how Christ fulfills her desires in ways that material possessions, social status, and worldly goals cannot. Then Ignatius presents the exercise on *the Standard of Christ*. The important insight here is that in order to appropriate the Standard of Christ and to consciously choose it, the retreatant must deepen the relationship with Christ to the point where she is identifying with Christ. This identification happens in a gradual process of exercises contemplating the life of Christ so as to gain knowledge of him and his vision for the humanity. These contemplations in their turn elicit the desire to love Christ more intimately and to follow him more closely. Here we see Ignatius's

---

29. Kolvenbach, *Road from La Storta*, 23.

theology of divine union at work: for Ignatius, divine union is achieved in the union of the human desire and God's desire for him or her, a desire that is realized in self-identification with Christ in the world. George Aschenbrenner observes that there is the process in which "Begging for our heart's true desire can gradually become so persistent that it draws us virtually into identification with that desire. . . . The process of identification is really a deepening union with God, now known in the yearning of our desire."[30]

To bring the retreatant to this identification with Christ, Ignatius follows the long tradition of Christian spiritual practice called *agere contra*, that is, to act against one's tendency toward making bad choices. The method of *agere contra* requires an analysis of the two opposing value systems, that of Satan, which consists of the desire for riches, honor and pride and leads to various vices (SpEx 142); and that of Christ, which consists of the desire for poverty, contempt and humility and leads to other virtues (SpEx 146). The tactic of Satan is to inspire fear in those who want to follow Christ.[31] In proposing riches, honor and pride as a standard of life, Satan implies that poverty, contempt and humility will result in fear. But *fear* restrains one from the *freedom to love and serve God*, the latter being precisely what the standard of Christ intends to propose. To embrace the value system of Christ is to live out the value of the Gospel he preaches, which presupposes one's experience of being loved by Christ. The Two Standards, therefore, presents two visions of the world and of human relationship to God, one based on fear (the standard of Satan), the other based on love (the standard of Christ).

Ignatian discernment is carried out by reflecting on and contemplating the biblical text and considering the context of one's life and the choice one wants to make in the light of the inspiration of the Holy Spirit. The hope is that through contemplation and in conversation with the help of a spiritual director, one begins to discern between the options so as to discover God's will in the choice he or she is about to make. The process is based on a set of rules for the discernment of spirits and rules for the discernment of God's will as indicated in the *Spiritual Exercises*. Ignatius categorizes spiritual movements into two types: *spiritual consolation* and *spiritual desolation*. The first movement generally comes from God or the good spirit. Its characteristics comprise a sense of peace and harmony, which ordinarily generates faith, hope and love of God, self and others. The other movement comes from the evil spirit and stirs the spirits opposite to those of the first movement: disturbance of peace, disharmony, lack of faith, hope and love

---

30. Aschenbrenner, "Becoming Whom We Contemplate," 37.
31. English, *Spiritual Freedom*, 148.

(SpEx 316–17). Consolation is further characterized by two types: *consolation with a cause* and *consolation without a preceding cause*. The first type has just been described. The second type has the characteristics of a mystical experience, what is commonly described as a "direct" experience of God. Ignatius describes "consolation without a preceding cause" as follows: "Only God our Lord can give the soul consolation without a preceding cause" (SpEx 330). This statement implies that the difference between *a consolation with a cause* and *a consolation without a preceding cause* lies in the phrase "without a preceding cause." Ignatius defines his usage: "by without a preceding cause, I mean without any previous perception or understanding of some object by means of which the consolation just mentioned might have been stimulated, through the intermediate activity of the person's acts of understanding and willing" (SpEx 330).

There is a significance of the term "previous" in the expression "consolation without a preceding cause." Any experience of God is mediated by a finite object or our reflection on it in some way. However, in the case of a consolation without a preceding cause, the cause exists, but it is *not previous* to the person who is having the experience. Here Ignatius is pointing to an experience he believes comes directly from God and not as a result of any finite object of one's immediate contemplation, nor as the result of the intellectual operation that brings about one's understanding and desire. God alone is the cause of an experience of a consolation without preceding cause; but the person, who is having an experience, does not have any knowledge of how the consolation comes about, except that it was giving to him directly from God.

In one sense, therefore, there is no need to discern the spiritual movement from within in the case of a consolation without a preceding cause, for it is clear that the experience is given by God. But such an experience of God, by nature, only happens to those who are disposed to it, and even then, the experience does not occur with great frequency. Many mystics agree that "direct" experience of God occurs on rare occasions. But even in such rare occasions when the experience does occur, the person who is experiencing it needs to be careful to observe the movement from the beginning to the end. If the movement from the beginning to the end originates in God and moves the person to faith, hope and love, then it is a *spiritual consolation*. But if the movement has changed its direction over time, then it is often the case the experience has turned into a *spiritual desolation*, even though the person may be deceived in thinking otherwise (SpEx 336).

Another important distinction must now be discussed: spiritual consolation and desolation are not mere human feelings and they don't always correspond to pleasure and pain. Michael Buckley observes:

> Consolation and desolation do not identify necessarily with pleasure and pain. Men with their arms locked, singing bawdy songs on their way to the local whorehouse, are in desolation for Ignatius [sic]: "any movement to base and earthly things." Consolation and desolation, then, must be critically distinguished both from Freud's description of instinctual satisfaction, and from the use of these terms in other spiritual authors. In no sense does consolation merge with pleasure and desolation with pain. They are obvious states of affectivity, but they are not denoted by their sensible or even spiritual enjoyment, but by their direction, by their terminus.[32]

Spiritual consolation can be confused with pleasure, and *spiritual desolation* can be mistaken for pain. However, in spiritual discernment it is crucial to know the difference between the two. Mere human feelings such as pleasure and pain can be part of a spiritual movement, but they are not its defining characteristic. A spiritual movement, in the true meaning of the term, must have either God or an evil spirit as their cause, or at least either God or the evil spirit affects the movement of the soul in a way that a mere human feeling does not. To discern the difference between *spiritual consolation* and *spiritual desolation* one should know the kind of feeling each movement stirs, but it is more important to recognize the direction to which each movement leads. The feeling attached to the spiritual movement functions only in the secondary sense. The primary task in spiritual discernment lies in the capability to recognize the different directions where the contrary movements are heading and to choose the direction that leads to God and life, while refusing the direction that leads to evil and destruction.

One cannot simply rely on the kind of feeling stirred in one to discern the direction of one's life. *Spiritual consolation* does not equate to pleasure, and *spiritual desolation* does not equate to sadness. A person who mourns the loss of a loved one certainly feels a sense of sadness, but if the sadness she feels is rooted in faith, hope and love for God and life, then it is a clear sign that the person is experiencing spiritual consolation, though it may appear to the observers that the person is experiencing spiritual desolation. The reverse is also true; namely, someone who may be energized and motivated for doing something he has perceived as good. But in the process if the person does not find deep and lasting joy in what he is doing, neither does he become more faith-filled, hopeful and loving, then the person should ask himself the question: Am I living in consolation, or have I already experienced desolation? In exploring the answer to this question, the person may

---

32. Buckley, "Structure of the Rules for the Discernment," 29.

realize that the experience he feels, may not in fact, be rooted in God's spirit, but perhaps it has been stirred by his own ambition and egoistic tendency which may have been suggested by the evil spirit. If that is the case, then the person has been deceived in thinking that he is experiencing *spiritual consolation* while in fact, the experience fits well with Ignatius's description of *spiritual desolation*.

A skillful contemplative, therefore, must be attentive to his or her spiritual movements, especially in times of consolation. Ignatius indicates that there are times when the evil spirit may appear like the good spirit, and when it does, even a person skilled in spiritual matter can be tricked into thinking that the spirit is indeed a good one. It was about this type of evil spirit that the Apostle Paul warned the Christians in Corinth, speaking of the false prophets. He says, "For such boasters are false prophets, deceitful workers, disguising themselves as apostles of Christ. And no wonder! Even Satan disguises himself as an angel of light. So it is not strange if his ministers also disguise themselves as ministers of righteousness. Their end will match their deeds" (2 Cor 11:13-15).

Paul cautions the Corinthians of the need to discern the good spirit from the bad spirit by observing the consequences that have been produced by the act, what we mean by the phrase, "Their end will match their deeds." In the same line of thought, Ignatius himself teaches that in the case of an experience of a consolation without preceding cause, it is the tactic of the evil spirit to disguise itself as the angel of light for the purpose of luring the person into its trap:

> It is characteristic of the evil angel, who takes on the appearance of an angel of light, to enter by going along the same way as the devout soul and then to exist by his own way with success for himself. That is, he brings good and holy thoughts attractive to such an upright soul and then strives little by little to get his own way, by enticing the soul over to his own hidden deceits and evil intentions (SpEx 332).

So to avoid being trapped by the deception of the evil spirit, one must observe the consequence of one's act: if the act has produced a bad consequence, then it is a clear indication that one has been manipulated by the evil spirit. That is why in discernment, basing oneself on spiritual movement alone is not sufficient; one must also carefully observe the direction in which that movement of spirit is heading. In case when one is not sure of the direction in which the movement is heading, one can always observe the consequence of one's act, because the act follows the movement as an effect follows its cause.

What happens in times of desolation? How should one go about discerning the various spiritual movements when one is experiencing *spiritual desolation*? As a general rule, Ignatius teaches that in times of desolation, one should not make any new decision nor change the decision that has already been made (SpEx 318). Rather, he or she should be patient with himself or herself, for patience in this case will enable him or her not to rush into making a decision that will be regretted later. Based on experience, Ignatius knows that consolation will indeed return, and he advises that one should wait for the return of consolation; then one can make a decision if need be (SpEx 321). Making a new decision or changing a previous decision in the case of an experience of desolation can only be a mistake, because in this case one is being misled by the evil spirit (SpEx 318).

Ignatius does not imply that in the case of desolation, one should not do anything except to wait for consolation to return. One of the chief causes of desolation, Ignatius teaches, is due to one's own laziness or negligence in the spiritual life. For this reason, Ignatius advises that one should make vigorous changes in himself or herself against desolation. For example, one should conduct a self-examination regarding thoughts and actions to see if they correlate to his or her spiritual and moral intuition and principle. It is also very profitable to read and meditate on the scriptures, particularly the psalms, and to be attentive to one's spiritual movements from within. All these are active ways to counter desolation while waiting for the return of consolation. Spiritual consolation will return, but it does not easily return without one's efforts to cultivate virtues and spiritual disciplines (SpEx 319 and 321).

One final point regarding making decision in times of desolation must be discussed. What if the desolation one is experiencing prolongs and seems not likely to go away anytime soon? What should one do in this case? Ignatius does not address this question directly, but the following description of desolation may give us a clue on why desolation may prolong. Allow me to cite Ignatius's text in its entirety here:

> When we are in desolation we should think that the Lord has left us to our own powers in order to test us, so that we may prove ourselves by resisting the various agitations and temptations of the enemy. For we can do this with God's help, which always remains available, even if we do not clearly perceive it. Indeed, even though the Lord has withdrawn from us his abundant fervor, augmented love, and intensive grace, he still supplies sufficient grace for our eternal salvation (SpEx 320).

The above description is not meant to be applicable universally. Spiritual endurance is different from one person to another, depending on one's current stage of spiritual development. Someone who is in an initial stage of spiritual life perhaps will not be able to endure spiritual desolation in the way Ignatius has described here. A person may be able to endure some suffering, but perhaps will not be able to resist the temptation to make a decision against the persisting suffering. On the other hand, someone who is advanced in spiritual life and who has had experienced desolation before and learned how to endure the suffering caused by desolation to further spiritual growth, will more likely be ready to accept the suffering caused by desolation.

To further explore the theme of spiritual desolation in spiritual life, let us turn to Saint Teresa of Avila (1515–82), a Carmelite mystic and contemporary of Saint Ignatius, particularly to the insights she offers in her most famous work, *Interior Castle*. In this work, Teresa describes the spiritual journey of the soul through seven dwelling places. The soul progresses from lower to higher stages of spiritual development. The first dwelling place focuses on the soul's self-knowledge in God. The process is twofold: the contemplative is encouraged to examine his or her own worldly affairs and disordered affections on the one hand, and to recognize God's love and mercy on the other hand. Teresa follows the long standing tradition of Christian spiritual practice which insists that only God's grace can reveal to one his or her sin, and only God can forgive and heal one's brokenness as a consequence of sin. But one must recognize and acknowledge one's dependence on God's love and mercy before healing can take place. In the second dwelling place, the contemplative begins develop habitual effort to turn away from committing serious sins, although he or she is not yet able to avoid venial (lesser serious) sin. In the third dwelling place, the contemplative is now able to habitually avoid venial sin. Teresa teaches that one should employ *mental prayer* in the first three dwelling places. That is, one should meditate on scriptural texts and other spiritual readings as well as meditate on the goodness and beauty of creation in these first three stages of spiritual progress. In the fourth and fifth dwelling places, the contemplative becomes much more reflective and introspective and thus is more attentive to God's Spirit. The distinctive characteristic of these two dwelling places can be in the way Teresa shifts the prayer method from mental prayer to *prayer of recollection*; the latter is characterized as a more quiet kind of meditation whereby the contemplative refrains from using scriptural texts and other external means in prayer; instead he or she listens more attentively to God's Spirit moving in his or her heart and becomes united with that Spirit. Thus in Teresa's fifth dwelling place, the prayer of union is introduced, although the contemplative only begins to experience union with God's Spirit at this stage. The fuller and more satisfactory experience of divine union does not take place until the seventh dwelling place, which is the final stage of the soul's journey to union with God in Teresa of Avila's *Interior Castle*.[33]

The most relevant point in our discussion of Teresa's seven dwelling places in her *Interior Castle* pertains to the sixth dwelling place. Teresa says that here in the sixth dwelling place the soul of the contemplative is engaged to the Lord Jesus Christ as in a betrothal. Jesus is the Spouse of the soul; and the soul, who has gone through the previous stages of spiritual growth, is now desiring to be completely united with its Spouse. It is in the desire for deeper intimacy with Jesus that the soul experiences suffering. It is not a suffering caused by self-pity, for the soul does experience Jesus's love. Rather, the suffering of the soul is perceived through its yearning to be in complete union with its Spouse on the one hand, and the feeling of the incompleteness, a "not yet" fulfillment of that union on the other hand. In other words, the characteristic feature of this stage of the soul is one of willingness and readiness to be tested for further growth in relationship with Jesus, its Spouse. The experience can be described as a kind of "bitter-sweet" condition within the soul. Teresa describes this condition as a *wound of love*: "The soul is now wounded with love for its Spouse and strives for more opportunities to be alone and, in conformity with its state, to rid itself of everything that can be an obstacle to this solitude."[34]

Needless to say, this kind of spiritual desolation is not meant for everyone. Rather, it is meant for those who have grown and become much advanced in the spiritual life. It is God who initiates this progress by giving the fervent soul the grace to endure suffering and to be tested by various trials. The soul may have a feeling that her Spouse has abandoned her. This, however, should not be taken literally. Rather, the Spouse is stretching the soul by temporarily withdrawing His presence from the soul, leaving her in search of consolation from other sources—for example, from a trusted friend, a spiritual director, or a priest—only the find out that they either disapprove her spiritual struggle and call it a deception in the spiritual life, or they are incapable of helping her. It is also typical that during this period of desolation, the soul's prayers become dry. This further intensifies the experience as an "unknowing" experience of love. The reason is that all natural faculties of the soul (sense, imagination, memory, will and intellect) are incapable of perceiving and understanding this spiritual phenomenon. Teresa, however, states that during these trails, the soul occasionally

---

33. Feldmeier, *Christian Spirituality*, 162–64.
34. Teresa of Avila, *Interior Castle*, 359.

experiences raptures from God. God makes occasional visits to the soul to comfort her and to strengthen her in her struggles with the test. It is through these struggles that the soul learns to put complete trust in God's mercy, for she realizes that if God has given her the grace to endure such sufferings for the sake of union with God, then it is only God can bring that desire to fulfillment. Teresa writes, "The best remedy... is to engage in external works of charity and to hope in the mercy of God who never fails those who hope in Him."[35] What is the outcome of this series of trials? Feldmeier's observation about Teresa's sixth dwelling place sums up her teaching: by stretching the soul in this way God allows her to be tested so as to learn to love God for God's sake rather than for its own spiritual comfort and sweetness.[36]

This insight into spiritual desolation is also mentioned by Ignatius in the *Spiritual Exercises*. There Ignatius shares the similar sentiment with that of Teresa. In one of the rules regarding spiritual desolation, Ignatius states that sometimes God allows the person to experience desolation so that he or she learns to stretch his or her love, service and praise of God without expecting consolation and increased graces in return (SpEx 322). Both Teresa of Avila and Ignatius of Loyola value spiritual suffering as a condition for spiritual growth. Suffering in the spiritual life is necessary for spiritual development. This statement should not be taken to imply that suffering is good in and of itself. Without a redemptive power of God in Jesus Christ, suffering becomes meaningless. At the same time, however, to avoid suffering at all costs will never result in spiritual growth.

Everyone appropriates suffering differently from anyone else, depending on one's spiritual condition and personal context. It must be stressed that not everyone is called to or capable of enduring suffering in the same way and to the same degree. In time of a prolonged desolation, therefore, it is advisable that one make a change in one's life so that the intensity caused by the prolonged suffering may diminish. The aim, however, is not to avoid suffering at all costs, but to create possibilities for a more balanced life, so that the enduring suffering does not become more and more prominent to the point of that it becomes unbearable. The method of *agere contra* (acting against one's tendency to give in to temptation) proved to be an effective way to counter prolonged desolation. It is not by accident that Teresa of Avila encourages those who are under the experience of a prolonged suffering to counter it by moving outward into serving others through works of charity. Ignatius of Loyola, too, would not advise that one sit in desolation;

---

35. Teresa of Avila, *Interior Castle*, 365.
36. Feldmeier, *Christian Spirituality*, 165.

rather, he strongly recommends that one pray more regularly and counter desolation by means of other devotional acts.

Thus far we have discussed discernment of spirits from the context of the Ignatian methods for discerning God's will based on the two main spiritual movements called *consolation* and *desolation*. But what if one must make a decision in times when she does not feel any spiritual movements? This is an important question to raise simply because to live means to make decisions, and decisions need to be made even when one does not feel strongly inclined towards one choice or another. How does one make a choice that is most conducive to the direction of one's life in God in this case?

In one of the rules for the discernment of God's will, Ignatius states that in such a case, one carefully considers the advantages and disadvantages of the available options, and then asks the question: To what option does my reason more incline? (SpEx 181–82). In suggesting the use of reason as the main faculty in discernment, Ignatius does not imply that rationality here functions as the sole capacity for making a choice. Rather, reason must be grounded in faith and the choice to be made needs to be confirmed by God's grace. The guiding question is always this: what one choice among others should I make, so that I may further grow in my relationship with God and better serve Him in serving others? The answer to this question can become more complex than one may have thought. When one does not feel inclined towards one choice or another, or when one feels that both choices present the same objective good, the choices appear arbitrarily. In such a case, Ignatius recommends that one imagine a situation when one takes on a role of a spiritual guide in giving advice to a person whom one has never met or known. Then imagine further how one would advise such a person to make a choice for the greater glory of God in such circumstance. Finally, one should apply the same advice to one's self and make a choice accordingly (SpEx 185). The exercise aims to provide objective criteria for considering and making a choice in time when one does not experience spiritual movements.

Chapter 3

Jesus Christ in the Contemplative Life

THE PRECEDING TWO CHAPTERS discussed the nature of contemplation and the role of spiritual discernment in contemplation. This chapter will present and discuss the centrality of Jesus Christ in the contemplative life. Its thesis is that Christian contemplation must be rooted in Jesus Christ and find fulfillment in him. Christian contemplation, as we understand it, aims to unite the human spirit with the Spirit of God. In the Christian faith, that union has been achieved in Jesus Christ, the Incarnation of God, through his life, suffering, death and resurrection. From this point of view, the human desire for divine union and the possibility to attain that union can only be found and fulfilled in Christ, because Christ is the *way* to God, the *truth* of God and the *life* in God (John 14:6).[1]

The present chapter has two divisions. In the first part, I will explore the Christian anthropology and the theology of the Incarnation, grounding them on the Christian doctrine of the Trinity and its implications for the Christian life. In the second part, I will discuss the Ignatian understanding of contemplation and present it as an illustration of a way to union with God in Jesus Christ.

---

1. Jesus says to his disciples, "I am the way, and the truth, and the life. No one comes to the Father except through me. If you know me, you will know my Father also. From now on you do know him and have seen him" (John 14:6–7).

THE CHRISTIAN GOD AS A PERSONAL GOD

Christians believe that human beings are created in the image and likeness of God (Genesis, 1:26). This belief implies that unlike any other of God's creatures, human beings are endowed with the desire for union with God and a capability to attain that union. It means that a human being is a *person* who possesses a capability for self-transcendence into the divine-likeness in a way that other creatures do not.

The significance of the term "person" as applied to humanity needs to be explored. An understanding of this term will shed light into how we appropriate Christian contemplation.

Our use of the word "person" has an unsuspected history and depth. The origin of the term "person" can be traced to the Christian doctrine of the Trinity. The Christian faith holds that the one God exists in three persons: Father, Son and Holy Spirit. The doctrine was formulated at the First Council of Constantinople in 381, but had a precursor at the Council of Nicaea in 325. The Church Fathers at the Council of Nicaea, in particular Saint Athanasius (296–373), employed the Greek term *hypostasis* to signify something common to each of the three persons of the one God, and thus to underscore their relational reality. *Hypostasis* means "mode of being." It is a word Athanasius used to denote the Trinity as the one God who exists in three different ways, or who has three different modes of being. Athanasius also employed the term *ousia*, which means "substance," to signify that in God there is one being. Both *hypostasis* and *ousia* refer to the divine essence of God who manifests in three different ways as Father, Son and Holy Spirit.

Athanasius's terminology enables him and the other Church's Fathers at the Council of Nicaea to argue for the divinity of the second person of the Trinity. By implication they argue for the divinity of Jesus Christ, the Incarnation of the second person of the Trinitarian God. According to the Fathers, the second person of the Trinity incarnates in Jesus, which means that even though Jesus has a human nature from his mother Mary, he is God by the divine nature, who exists as a divine *hypostasis* from eternity. In other words, Jesus is God in the flesh; he is the divine Son of the Trinity.[2] This was the Fathers' direct response to Arius (256–336), who had denied the divinity of the second person of the Trinity and thus ushered in what has been commonly known as the "Arian controversy." Athanasius and the other Fathers at the Nicene Council rejected the Arian view and deemed it heretical.

---

2. Davis, *First Seven Ecumenical Council (325–787)*, 62–63.

Fifty-six years later, at the First Council of Constantinople in 381, the Fathers of the Church employed the Athanasian terminology to argue for the divinity of the Holy Spirit. Prior to the Council, there existed the Semi-Arian movement which denied the divinity of the Holy Spirit. To counter this movement, the Fathers stated that the Holy Spirit "proceeds from the Father and the Son and with the Father and the Son He is adored and glorified."[3] This creedal phrase signifies that the divine substance (*ousia*) exists as the Holy Spirit, the third person (*hypostasis*) of the Trinity.

The doctrine of the Trinity, therefore, declares the divine substance of each of the three persons of the one God, as Blessed John Henry Newman indicates, "The Father is the One Eternal Personal God; the Son is the One Eternal Personal God; and the Holy Spirit is One Eternal Personal God."[4] At the same time, each of the Persons of the Trinity exists and manifests in a way that the other two Persons do not.[5]

In essence, the doctrine of the Trinity teaches us about a relational and communal God. The God of Christianity is essentially a God whose nature is unity, but it is a unity that exists in diversity, so that the essence of the Trinitarian God must be perceived as the divine relational and communal reality. In other words, there cannot be a multiplicity of consciousness in God, even though the divine consciousness may be manifested in three different ways. Karl Rahner (1904–1984) expounded the unity in the Trinitarian God as follows:

> There is in God a knowledge of these three persons (hence in each person about himself and about the two other persons), a knowledge about the Trinity both as *consciousness* and as "object" of knowledge (as known). But there are not three consciousnesses; rather, the one consciousness subsists in a threefold way. There is only one real consciousness in God, which is shared by Father, Son, and Spirit, by each in his own proper way. Hence the threefold subsistence is not qualified by three consciousnesses. The "subsistence" itself is as such not "personal," if we understand this word in the modern sense. The "distinctness" of the persons is not constituted by a distinctness of conscious subjectivities, nor does it include the latter. This distinctness is conscious. However, it is not conscious for three subjectivities, but it is the awareness of this distinctness in one only real consciousness.[6]

3. Cited from the Nicene-Constantinopolitan Creed.
4. Newman, *Essay in Aid of a Grammar of Assent*, 119.
5. Newman, *Essay in Aid of a Grammar of Assent*, 119.
6. Rahner, *Trinity*, 106–7.

For Rahner, God exists as a unity-in-relations; the relations flow from the unity of the one divine nature who possesses a single consciousness. The differences among the three persons of God must be perceived as relative and not essential differences. The three persons of the same God are aware of their one consciousness, which is possessed by them in three different ways. This means that what is conscious in one person of the Trinity is also known by the other two persons, so that in God there is always a union of consciousness.

Rahner clarifies that the divine consciousness, obviously, cannot be applicable to human beings. Being creatures, human beings do not possess the divine consciousness. This means that what is conscious in one human person is not necessarily known by others unless the consciousness becomes manifested through a person's speech, choice and action. And even when it is manifested, the manifestation of human consciousness ultimately depends on the conditions posed by the existential reality, and thus is always limited. Be that as it must, the term "person," as we have discussed it, sheds light on how we should understand the divine-human relationship on the one hand, and the human relationship on the other.

To be a person means to be a self-conscious *subject*, not in the same sense as the three persons of God are to one another, but in an analogous sense. To be a human person implies that he or she possesses a capability for an awareness of his or her own intellectual and volitional operation. Unlike animals and other animated beings, a person is unique in that he or she not only is aware of the surroundings through the external senses, but, as a *subject* who is aware of his or her awareness. A person can reflect on the information received by the senses, and through a self-reflective process, he or she understands and evaluates the information and thus can make a choice about it. For example, human experience of joy and pain teaches us that as human beings we not only feel joy or pain when these things occur to us, but we can reflect on them and distinguish their causes, movements and consequences so as to detect their meanings and implications and to react appropriately. This self-reflective process indicates that inherent in human beings is the capability for a self-awareness which enables us to be reflective and intentional about our choices and actions in a way that animals cannot.

To further explore the concept of "person as subject" let us turn to Bernard Lonergan (1904–84). In his book, *The Subject*, Lonergan calls the human person an "immanentist subject," that is a subject whose capability for self-transcendence is inherent. By the term "subject" Lonergan also means that a person is not a mere "object" to which things happen and from which an action flows in a non-purposeful way. Rather, as a "subject" a person can reflect on what has occurred and find meaning from it in the same sense we just discussed. Lonergan observes, "The subject is within but he does not remain totally within. His knowing involves an intentional self-transcendence."[7] This self-transcendence occurs in an act of knowing where knowledge is gained in a gradual manner: from recalling or confronting one's own experience of a phenomenon, to reflecting on one's own experience so as to understand it, to evaluating and making a judgment pertaining to one's findings, and finally to making a choice about what and how to act in the light of one's new knowledge about the phenomenon under study. For Lonergan, human knowledge involves a gradual process of reflection, evaluation and decision. In every step of this gradual development, the person is aware of his or her own intellectual, moral, and religious operations.

In Lonergan's *Method*, there exists another level of consciousness and operation beyond the four discussed: It is when one is conscious of the divine love in one's act of experiencing, understanding, judging and acting. It is here at this highest level of human consciousness that a person unites with the divine who is at work in the world. The divine union, once achieved at this highest level of human consciousness, enables the person to embody God's Spirit in the world and find fulfillment in it.[8]

GRACE AS THE BASIS FOR HUMAN SELF-TRANSCENDENCE

The question must now be raised: If human beings are created for union with God, and if God is transcendent while human beings are created, then how can human beings attain union with God? The question implies that divine union presupposes communication between human and divine. But it is impossible for human beings to fully comprehend divine communication. Hence, if human knowledge of the divine is possible at all, it must be a knowledge revealed by God. In other words, the human process toward divine union presupposes grace.

But what exactly is grace? And what is the relationship between grace and human nature? The answers to these questions have already been implied in our discussion thus far, for we have established that to be human is to be created in the image and likeness of God, which implies that human beings are made capable for divine union. But the mode of union with the divine is achieved by divine revelation, though not without human response.

---

7. Lonergan, *Subject*, 13.

8. I refer the reader to Lonergan's book, *Method in Theology* for the full discussion of Lonergan's understanding of the human person as a "subject" and his view on human knowledge as "self-transcendence."

This means that grace cannot be something foreign to human beings; rather, grace is a constitutive element of the human person. For if grace exists as the necessary condition for divine union, then grace also exists as the ground of human transcendence into God's likeness. Indeed, Karl Rahner would say that grace is a constitutive principle of what it means to be a human person.[9] "Man should be able to receive this Love which is God himself; he must have a congeniality for it. He must be able to accept it (and hence grace, the beatific vision) as one who has room and scope, understanding and desire for it. Thus he must have a real "potency" for it. He must have it always."[10] The same view is shared by Henri de Lubac in his book, *The Mystery of the Supernatural*, where Lubac insists that it is impossible to conceive the notion of "pure nature" in reference to human nature. For Lubac, the notion of "pure nature," in a modern sense of the word, is something not considered at all in the theology of the early Church, least of all in the eastern tradition.[11] But even in the western tradition, Saint Augustine of Hippo (354–430), for example, shares the view that human nature is infused with grace. We observe this trend of theology in one of Augustine's most famous sayings, "You have made us for yourself, and our heart is restless until it rests in you."[12] The restlessness of the human heart, in the Augustinian sense, reveals the ever-yearning longing for something beyond itself, and that "beyond" is nothing other than God who is the Source of life and love, experienced at the depth of the human heart. But if this human yearning for the divine is inherent, then grace must exist as a constitutive principle of the human person.

To further explore the relationship between nature and grace, let us turn to the second account of creation in the book of Genesis. There we are told that "God formed man from the dust of the ground, and breathed into his nostrils the breath of life, and the man became a living being."[13] This intimate account of God's creation of humanity shows that God does not create human beings as something utterly different from God. Rather, God creates them in an act of self-emptying in love. God pours out God's very life into human lives, and thus, human beings become the embodiments of God's flowing of life and love. Perhaps Saint Augustine's saying, cited earlier, was inspired by this account of God's creation of humanity, in that the human heart is restless because its very breath (or its spirit) comes from God and can only be satisfied by God's Spirit. For when God creates a human being

---

9. See Rahner, *Foundations of Christian Faith*, 116.
10. Rahner, "Relationship between Nature and Grace," 187.
11. Lubac, *Mystery of the Supernatural*, 5.
12. Chadwick, *Saint Augustine Confessions*, 3.
13. Gen 2:7.

with God's own breath, doesn't it mean that God creates him or her with the very Spirit of God? And if the Spirit of God is present in human being as a constituent element, as have said, then is not human being a being that is distinctly created by God for the sake of divine union?

According to the Christian tradition, the human soul exists forever, even though the body dies and is thus destroyed. The creedal statement in regards to the afterlife also asserts that there will be the resurrection of the body to be united with the soul, for the soul would be incomplete without a body. This creedal statement points to the consistent truth that human union with the divine begins in this life and continues into the afterlife. Seen from this perspective, divine union should be perceived as a human destiny and implies a journey. That journey starts right here and now in this life and continues to progress into eternity. To be united with God means to live in God's Spirit right here and right now. To the extent that the human spirit is united with the Spirit of God, human beings become God's embodiments in the world. The purpose of God's creation of humanity in God's own image and likeness really means that human beings are the reflection of God in the world; in other words, an image reflects the Image. Because human beings are created with the very Spirit of God, human self-transcendence into the divine likeness is realized in direct proportion to the divine manifestation of grace in and through human beings. The more the person grows into the life of God, the more he becomes true to his nature, and the more he becomes true to his nature, the more he mediates God's divine reality in the world. Viewed from this perspective, the dignity of a human person becomes clear: he is created with a capacity for divine union, and that capacity implies a vocation to cooperate with God in bringing about and accomplishing God's dream for the world.

PRIDE AS THE ROOT OF HUMAN SIN

Human experience, however, reveals the reality sin. "Being created in the image and likeness of God" implies that human beings should have realized their capability for union with God and lived according to their knowledge so as to fulfill their purpose. But instead, as we are told in chapter three of Genesis, Adam and Eve, our first parents, disobeyed God's command. Eve was tempted by the serpent to eat the "forbidden fruit," which God had ordered her and Adam not to eat. The reason provided by the serpent was appealing and attractive to Eve. The serpent said to her, "God knows that when you eat of the fruit your eyes will be open, and you will be like God, knowing good and evil."[14] Seeing that the fruit was beautiful and that by eating it she would possess the knowledge similar to God's, Eve decided to eat the fruit. She also gave it to her husband, Adam, and he ate it. The moment they both ate the forbidden fruit, their eyes were indeed open; and they recognized their nakedness and felt shameful before God, and so they made loincloths to cover themselves.[15]

The above biblical account reveals the nature of sin and the human condition as a consequence of sin. Even though a human person is created in the image and likeness of God and endowed with the very breath of God, nonetheless, God's act of creation of a human person is a free gift. Because it is a free gift, it must be received by the person's freedom. Only in total freedom can human beings come into a true and meaningful relationship with God, whose freedom initiates the divine-human relationship. However, just as human knowledge is limited and cannot fully comprehend the nature of God, so too, human freedom is a created freedom, and as such it is not an absolute freedom. Human freedom is conditioned by the concrete reality of life and thus is limited. Adam and Eve should have chosen to obey God's command rather than to commit an act of disobedience against God in eating the "forbidden fruit." But the human limited freedom reveals another aspect of human condition, namely, human beings are capable of sin.

Furthermore, Adam and Eve's disobedience to God reveals that pride is at the root of their sin. In other words, sin is an act in which human beings cross the line between God and humanity; it is a refusal to acknowledge God as the Creator and to accept oneself as a creature. The root of sin is pride and it implies a contradiction: If grace manifests in a direct proportion of human cooperation with God so that the more the person is infused with grace the more she becomes like God, the opposite can be said of sin, in that sin reverses the direction of life in grace. The more the person lives in sin, the more she becomes disconnected with God. In that state, she is not capable of realizing her true self, and consequently, she lives in isolation from others. In other words, sin denies God as the Creator, and when that happens, divine union becomes impossible. Consequently, human life results in fragmentation.

JESUS CHRIST AS THE SAVIOR OF HUMANITY

Since God created human beings for life in union with God, God would not leave them in the condition of sin. Rather, God restores them to the

14. Gen 3:4–5.
15. Gen 3:6–7.

original image with which God created them. The Incarnation of God in Jesus becomes the turning point in the history of God's salvation precisely because, through his life, suffering, death and resurrection, Christ was able to reverse the human tendency toward sin and restore the human image to the likeness of God. Seen from this point of view, the creation of humanity in the image and likeness of God destines humanity for a supernatural end which is a life in union with God in Christ. The Incarnation of God in Jesus reiterates and deepens the understanding of God's purpose in creating human beings; namely, union with God. That union has now become possible through the grace of Christ. In this sense, the Incarnation of God in Jesus revealed the fullness of God's revelation to humanity, a revelation initiated by God's creation of the world and of human beings for the purpose of God-becoming-human in order to bring God's revelation to a completion.

This line of thought has been laid out by Henri de Lubac as follows: "The fact that the nature of spiritual beings, as it actually exists, is not conceived as an order destined to close in finally upon itself, but in a sense open to an inevitably supernatural end."[16] Here Lubac is referring to the twofold creation of humanity. He calls the first "natural creation" in that God creates human beings in God's image and likeness; it is the creation from the earth, from matter. The second creation is called "spiritual creation," precisely because it is given by the grace of Jesus Christ. The first creation gives man life as a spiritual being distinct from other kinds of living beings. But it is in the second creation, which is a creation in a new life in Christ, that a person finds his or her fulfillment, because it is in Christ that a human person becomes elevated to the life in union with God, which otherwise would have been impossible. Human beings misuse and abuse God's first creation in committing sin, as we just said, but Christ restores the image of God in man and brings about a second creation of humanity in Him. This theology is inspired by the words of Saint Paul in his first letter to the Corinthians where Paul says,

> But in fact Christ has been raised from the dead, the first fruits of those who have died. For since death came through a human being, the resurrection of the dead has also come through a human being; for as all die in Adam, so all will be made alive in Christ. But each in his own order: Christ the first fruits, then at his coming those who belong to Christ.[17]

The distinction between the two types of creation and their interdependence sheds light into how we appropriate God's eternal plan of salvation.

16. Lubac, *Mystery of the Supernatural*, 31.
17. 1 Cor 15:20–22.

The relationship between grace and human nature once more becomes elucidated. In one sense, grace is distinct from nature, and thus, the distinction must be maintained. To blur the distinction between grace and nature inevitably leads to sin, as was discussed in the case of Adam and Eve. But, as we asserted, grace is also constitutive of human beings in that God created human beings in God's image and likeness, and God did so with God's own Spirit. We have seen how both Karl Rahner and Henri de Lubac share this line of thought. But Lubac's description of human beings as "spiritual beings destined for a supernatural end," coupled with the distinction between "natural creation" and "spiritual creation," are an important development in the understanding of sin and salvation. From the reality of sin we learn that human nature as understood in the first creation is not yet a "perfect nature." It was created for union with God, but that union cannot be attained unless it is elevated by the grace of God in Jesus Christ. In other words, the creation of humanity in God's image and likeness destines human beings for the final goal: union with God in Christ. But this final goal was obstructed by sin. The Incarnation of God in Jesus becomes necessary to restore human dignity. Jesus Christ was conceived by the Virgin Mary through the Power of the Holy Spirit. Hence his human nature was exempted from the original sin of Adam and Eve, so that the human nature could be restored in him.

The question, "Why did God become human?" has already been answered by the Fathers of the Church. For example, Saint Athanasius said that "God becomes man in order that man might become God."[18] A similar statement can be found in Saint Augustine: "To make those who were men gods, he who was God was made man."[19] Both statements underscore the mystery of God as the God who does not remain distant from human beings, but who, through God's Son, has become human and dwells among us.[20]

The phrase "God becoming human in Jesus" signifies that God decided to "lower" God's status as a Transcendent Being in an act of self-emptying-in-love for humanity. The language of "God becoming human," therefore, ought to be interpreted from the Mystery of God's love for humanity; otherwise why would God become human? God wants to be human so that God can relate to human beings in way that they can understand, and in doing so human beings can appropriate God's way of being in the world. It is the only way for human beings to be transformed into God.

---

18. Lubac, *Mystery of the Supernatural*, 135.
19. Lubac, *Mystery of the Supernatural*, 135.
20. John 1:14.

The letter to the Hebrews attests to the reason of God becoming human in the following words: "Long ago God spoke to our ancestors in many and various ways by the prophets, but in these last days he has spoken to us by a Son."[21] Indeed, God's revelation was made known to the human family through the law and the prophets of the Old Testament, but there is a personal revelation of God in Jesus to which the law and the prophets cannot compare. The two modes of revelation are not contrary to each other. The law and the prophets speak to the people on God's behalf. They comprise an essential part of the formation of the people of God. Through them God teaches the people and form them into a religious and holy people. But there is an essential difference between the letters of the law and the words of the prophets, which are inspired by God's Spirit, and their living manifestation in Jesus Christ, the divine person in the human flesh. Human language can express that which is divinely inspired, but the written word of God by human hands cannot fully comprehend the mystery of God, and thus cannot effectively convey the full meaning of God's communication to the human family. The mode of human encounter of the divine in Jesus Christ occurs in a way more personal than that of the law and the prophets. In and through Jesus, human beings are able to relate to God in a more concrete and experiential way, because Jesus not only teaches people about God as if the revelation still remains in written form, but he relates to God in his prayer and he treats other people as God would treat them with love, compassion, mercy and inclusiveness. In doing so, Jesus embodies his teaching in his own person. The written words become a living reality in him, something the law and the prophets of the Old Testament could not achieve. It is in this sense that Jesus spoke in reference to himself in the Gospel of Matthew, that he did not come to abolish the law and the prophets but to fulfill them (Matt 5:17).

But the relationship between the Old and New Testaments needs further exploration in order to shed light into our present discussion on the role of Jesus Christ in God's salvific plan. We may want to raise the questions: Why did God delay in coming? In other words, why was there a need for the law and the prophets as a preparation for the coming of Jesus? Wouldn't it have been more beneficial to the human family if God incarnated earlier?

We cannot sufficiently answer these questions because the human mind cannot fully comprehend God's eternal plan of salvation of humanity. But the hope is that in exploring the answers to these questions we will better appropriate the relationship between the law and the prophets of the Old Testament and their fulfillment in Jesus Christ.

---

21. Heb 1:1–2.

In the Gospel of Luke we are told that Jesus was handed the scroll of the Prophet Isaiah where it was written: "The Spirit of the Lord is upon me, because he has anointed me to bring good news to the poor. He has sent me to proclaim release to the captives and recovery of sight to the blind; to let the oppressed go free; and to proclaim the year of the Lord's favor."[22] After reading these words to the people in the synagogue, Jesus says, "Today this scripture has been fulfilled in your hearing."[23] Jesus is referring to himself as the fulfillment of the law and the prophets, a fulfilment that could not have been brought about earlier because human beings would not have been able to receive God's revelation in Jesus. God's revelation presupposes human response, and human response to divine revelation presupposes human recognition of God's intention. In other words, the human mind must be prepared for God's revelation in Christ, and the preparatory process must occur in stages whereby each stage corresponds to the appropriate level of human mental development. Saint Chrysostom (347–407), one of the Fathers of the Church, addresses God's formation of humanity in the following words:

> In religion, as in human learning, we need a gradual introduction, beginning by the more easily learned matters and the first elements. The Creator comes to our aid so that our eyes, accustomed to darkness, may be gradually opened to the full light of truth. He has arranged all things in view of our weakness; he trains us first to perceive the shadow of objects and the sun's reflection in the water so that we are not blinded by direct contact with its rays: the Mosaic law was the shadow of things to come, and the teaching of the prophets was the truth in a form which was still obscure.[24]

God becomes human in Jesus at the time in human history when the human consciousness has been raised to the level fitting for the revelation of God in human flesh. Not only had the human desire for God been purified through the Jewish religious Law and the words of the prophets, but also the human mind had evolved to the level capable of comprehending conceptual reality of the created world and the spiritual world and their relationship, as can be seen in Hellenistic philosophy. All these precursors were parts of the natural progress toward human maturity before the coming of God in the flesh. Henri de Lubac observes, "If the salvation offered by God is in fact the salvation of the human race, since this human race lives and develops in

---

22. Luke 4:18–19.
23. Luke 4:21.
24. Lubac, *Catholicism*, 250.

time, any account of this salvation will naturally take a historical form—it will be the history of the penetration of humanity by Christ."[25] God became human when human beings had been prepared to receive God in the flesh.

From this perspective, we can affirm that the Incarnation of God exists in the eternal plan of God's creation and redemption. In God's act of creation of the world, God has already communicated with humanity. The first account of creation in the book of Genesis tells us that after God had created all living beings on the earth, God created human beings in God's image and likeness. Then God blessed human beings and entrusted to them the care of all things that God had created.[26] So God creates in order to give life to creation, and God creates human beings in God's image and likeness so that they may become God's co-creators in bringing God's creation to a completion. Just as Jesus Christ reveals God in the flesh and thus he fulfills the law and the prophets, so too human beings, through participating in the grace of Christ, can manifest the Spirit of Christ in the world.

CREATION AND REDEMPTION

Seen from this perspective, creation and redemption go hand in hand, and both reveal the Mystery of God as the God of love. God is love, and the creating act of God is implied by God's love. But if God is love, and God creates from love, then what is creation but love itself? Perhaps it is in this sense that Karl Rahner says, "The *economic* Trinity is the *immanent* Trinity and the *immanent* Trinity is the *economic* Trinity."[27] By this, Rahner means that the Trinitarian life of God's inner reality has been revealed to the human family by God's action. Because of God's act of creation the human family has now belonged to the household of God. God's act of creation of humanity signifies that humanity does not exist as a mere extension of God, but intrinsically relates to God; so much so that human beings can embody God's Spirit in the world. The process of human development forever depends on God's grace, and to the extent that God's grace can be appropriated by human beings and becomes manifested in the world, God's inner reality is revealed. In other words, human beings are created in God's own image and likeness and are destined to union with God. But that union implies God's desire to reveal God's self to human beings and through human beings to the world. Human transcendence is conditioned by the divine revelation and vice versa.[28]

25. Lubac, *Catholicism*, 141.
26. Gen 1:26–31.
27. Rahner, *Trinity*, 22.
28. Rahner, *Trinity*, 55.

In her book, *God for Us*, Catherine Mowry LaCugna (1952–1997) explains Rahner's interconnection between *immanent* and *economic* Trinity. She argues that "The doctrine of the Trinity, properly understood, is the affirmation of God's intimate communication with us through Jesus Christ in the Holy Spirit."[29] The key word in LaCugna's statement is "communication." The Christian God is a communicable God; that is, God exists as three persons: Father, Son, and Holy Spirit who relate to one another in a personal way. This is what Rahner means by the term "immanent" in reference to the Trinitarian God. But by creating human beings in God's own image and likeness, God desires to share God's very life with human beings in way that they can relate and respond to. Consequently, God's communication must now take on a different mode: it is a divine revelation through human mediation. This mode of divine revelation corresponds to Rahner's *economic* reality of the Trinitarian God.

The Mystery of the Trinity can only be seen from the Mystery of the Incarnation and both need to be perceived from the Mystery of God's creation and salvation. The Trinitarian God exists as a communion of love, and love is not static but dynamic. Love moves out in search for the beloved. Saint John says, "God is love, and those who abide in love abide in God, and God abides in them."[30] God is not self-contained. Rather, God creates in order to share love with creatures. Just as the Trinity is a communion of the three divine persons in unity and love, so too the human family, though diverse in members, forms a community of persons whose lives can be in communion with God and with one another. The communal dimension of the Christian faith originates with the Trinity, reveals itself in Jesus, and manifests in the Church. Catherine LaCugna conveys the essence of the Trinitarian God and the implication of God for humanity in the following words:

> The doctrine of the Trinity is ultimately therefore a teaching not about the abstract nature of God, nor about God in isolation from everything other than God, but a teaching about God's life with us and our life with each other. Trinitarian theology could be described as par excellence a theology of relationship, which explores the mysteries of love, relationship, personhood and communion within the framework of God's self-revelation in the person of Christ and the activity of the Spirit.[31]

The word "love" in reference to God can be used interchangeably with the word "life"; and in this sense we can say that God creates human beings

---

29. LaCugna, *God for Us*, ix.
30. 1 John 4:16.
31. LaCugna, *God for Us*, 1.

in order to give them life. Through their own misuse of the will, human beings refuse the God of life and commit sins against God. Sin, therefore, leads to human self-destruction. What happens is that sin disrupts the movement toward human spiritual development, and thus sin interrupts the human progress towards union with the God of life. The redemptive grace of Christ reverses the human sinful tendency and regenerates the capability for human self-transcendence. Every time a person turns away from sin and moves toward Christ, he is renewed in Christ's Spirit. The redemptive power Christ brought for us is an everlasting power. That power effects in us an ongoing redemption in that it re-creates us anew in Christ and transforms us into a new creation in him. Thomas Rausch observes,

> It makes much sense theologically to see creation as ongoing, nature as both damaged by sin and graced, and the Spirit gathering us now and in the future into the paschal mystery of Christ's dying and rising to everlasting life. Creation is not an event in the past; if God were not sustaining us in this very instant, we would simply cease to exist. Nor is salvation only a future event, individualistically understood as our being "saved" and entering into bliss. Salvation is God's grace transforming us now and giving us in the Spirit a participation in the divine life.[32]

To perceive creation and salvation as an ongoing act of God entails the communal life that we have, a life rooted in the Trinity. This means that God creates each of us personally, which implies that the process of salvation must take place personally in each one of us. To be a person means to be a "subject" in the sense we discussed in the first part of this chapter. Only a person can appropriate God's grace and respond to God in true freedom. However, as we discussed, God exists in unity, and God creates for the sake of union with God. So in an ultimate sense, the whole creation comes from God and will be united in God as a whole. This means that the communal dimension of the human life is essential to what it means to be human, and salvation in God too must have the communal dimension. That is why Christians pray for the departed souls in purgatory as well as to the saints in heaven for their intercession.

IGNATIAN CONTEMPLATION

Our discussion thus far on Christian anthropology and the theology of the Incarnation sets the context for our discussion on Ignatian contemplation.

---

32. Rausch, *This Is Our Faith*, 94.

In this second part of the chapter I will present the theology of the *Spiritual Exercises* of Saint Ignatius of Loyola (1491–1556), by centering on his understanding of contemplation as "contemplative in action." In the preceding chapter, I briefly presented Saint Ignatius of Loyola along with Saint Teresa of Avila. There I discussed the reality of the soul's suffering as the necessary condition for spiritual growth. In comparing and contrasting the two mystics' views of the soul's experience of the absence of God, I highlighted the similarity between Teresa and Ignatius by indicating that for both mystics, the experience of God's "seeming absence" teaches the soul to realize her need for God and her love of God for God's sake rather than for her own spiritual gratification. At the same time, I underscored the difference between the two mystics' approaches to the state of divine union. For Teresa, in the final dwelling place, which is the final stage of the soul's union with God, the soul experiences the ongoing presence of God which enables the lower part of the soul to continue engaging in the daily activity while the spiritual part of the soul constantly contemplates God. In this sense, Teresa's stage of divine union could be described as "contemplative in action" even though her spirituality comprises one of the strictest forms of contemplative life, highly valuing the reclusive way of life dedicated to contemplation. In contrast, we see a different approach to contemplation in Ignatius of Loyola. For Ignatius, contemplation of God ought to be manifested in action, as can be seen in the preliminary observation Ignatius makes at the beginning of the exercise on the "Contemplation to Attain Love." There Ignatius states, "Love ought to manifest itself more by deeds than by words" (SpEx 230). For Ignatius, our love of God manifests in our love for others. The latter manifests and completes the former.

Now the theme of Christian love of God and neighbor has already been expressed in the New Testament. For example, Jesus says, "Truly I tell you, just as you did it to one of the least of these who are members of my family, you did it to me" (Matt 25:40); and conversely, "Truly I tell you, just as you did not do it to one of the least of these, you did not do it to me" (Matt 25:45). This teaching of Jesus comes from his parable about the Final Judgment Day, where it is implied that people will be judged based on their love, or lack thereof, for their brothers and sisters. The teaching reinforces Jesus's teaching on the Double Commandment, where he says, "You shall love the Lord your God with all your heart, and with all your soul, and with all your mind. This is the greatest and first commandment. And a second is like it: You shall love your neighbor as yourself" (Matt 22:37–39).

On the one hand, the love of God and the love of the others are not the same love, for God and creatures are distinct from each other; they exist as two different objects of human love. However, the two objects of love cannot be perceived as separate from each other. God's own breath of life creates us. And what is this very breath of God but love, for God is love? (1 John 4:7). So our experience of true love can be grasped and described as the experience of the divine life that is flowing in us. We are able to love others; thanks to the inspiration of the divine love we have appropriated. This is the *Transcendental Love*, which Lonergan describes as the human capacity for self-transcendence in the fifth level of consciousness. This kind of love comes as a gift from God and it is perceived with an eye of faith in the God of love. It is essentially different from other kinds of human love. Tad Dunne observes, "Religious faith goes beyond friendship and family love. Religious faith originates in an orientation which we experience *before* we know God, while the eye of friendly love originates in the love that follows *after* we know a friend. Faith regards even human love from the vantage point of transcendent love."[33] So the Double Commandment regarding the love of God and the love of neighbor ought to be seen as one commandment of love, for both the love of God and the love of neighbor, in the true meaning of the word, originates in the same *Transcendent Love* who is God.

We see then that our true love for others flows from and reflects God's love for them. The two loves cannot be separated. Saint John expresses the interlock between the two types of love quite bluntly when he says, "Those who say, 'I love God,' and hate their brothers or sisters, are liars; for those who do not love a brother or sister whom they have seen cannot love God whom they have not seen. The commandment we have from him [Jesus] is this: those who love God must love their brothers and sisters also" (1 John 4:20–21).

Furthermore, Christian love, in the sense of Lonergan's *Transcendent Love* as we discussed it, is essentially a dynamic movement, a potential that reveals itself in action. Divine love manifests in deeds more than in words, as Ignatius said. Even in human love, we know that when we love someone or something, it is because that someone or something has become the object of the desire of our will. So every desire of the will has a corresponding object. The desire of the will cannot be satisfied unless it has found its object. It is in seeking for the object of love that the desire of the will moves outward into action, for it is only in the act that the desire of the will finds its fulfillment.

In an analogous way we can talk about the love of God. If God's essence is love, and if love always moves out in search for the beloved, then God's act of creation should not be conceived as a consequence of God's love as if it were an afterthought of God. Rather, God's creation is conceived

---

33. Dunne, *Lonergan and Spirituality*, 119–20.

from the point of view of God's eternal love. The Greek word *eros* captures the meaning of God's love for creatures. In Plato's meaning of the word, *eros* is the experience of the "not enough" or the "there is more," which implies the lover's desire to create in order to love that which is created.[34] God creates us to give us life. In creating us, God not only shows how God loves us, but God also reveals to us that God's essence is reflected in God's creation. We can be transformed into the love of God because we are created for that purpose. Seen from this view, when we say that human beings are created in the image and likeness of God, we in truth acknowledge that in using our gifts and talents to cooperate with God's grace we are, in fact, bringing God's love to the world; and in doing so, we are being created and find our fulfillment. So the initial act of God's creation by giving us life makes possible for us to cooperate with God's love for the world. In this sense, our cooperation with God's grace becomes our participation in God's eternal plan of creation and salvation.

At this juncture in our discussion, I want to refer to Ignatius's second observation as found in the "Contemplation to Attain Love," to explore what contemplation in action really means. Ignatius says, "Love consists in a mutual communication between the two persons. That is, the one who loves gives and communicates to the beloved what he or she has, or a part of what one has or can have; and the beloved in return does the same to the lover. Thus, if the one has knowledge, one gives it to the other who does not; and similarly in regard to honors or riches. Each shares with the other" (SpEx 231). We have seen how Ignatius insisted on the deeds of our love for others rather than on mere words. But what should our actions consist of? What are their characteristics?

If we return to Lonergan's four levels of knowing: experience, understanding, judging and acting, we see that these levels are built on each other and return to each other for affirmation of what is known. All knowledge begins with the senses and ends in the intellect, as Thomas Aquinas would have said. Lonergan's first level of knowledge is based on the experience of the sense data. At this level we need to be *attentive* to the information we receive through the senses, e.g., knowledge gained by watching the news, reading books, listening to a lecture, or conducting interviews. Once we have accumulated sufficient information pertaining to the object of our study, then we need to examine the information through careful analysis of the different components, arguments and cases presented in it, and by comparing and contrasting the various aspects and viewpoints. In all this Lonergan insists that we be *intelligent* in our attempt to carry out the

---

34. See Dunne, *Lonergan and Spirituality*, 80.

investigation. Then there is a process in which we make value judgment regarding our findings in order to make a *reasonable* choice about them. Finally, after we have made the decision on the right and wrong, the good and bad pertaining to the case, then we need to act on it. Our act becomes a well-informed act, because it is based from our well-informed conscience and intentionality. In this condition, we can become more *responsible* for our action.[35]

If we match Lonergan's four levels of human knowing with our discussion on Ignatian "contemplative in action," we can observe a similarity between the two theologians. When Ignatius insisted that love ought to manifest itself more in deeds than in words, he implied that our deeds ought to be based on the reality in which we live, enlightened by our thoughtful analysis and informed by our value judgment. That is why Ignatius insisted on our need to further discern our gifts and talents and to use them in the service of God by serving others. In other words, the service we offer others must flow from the love of God that we have experienced through prayer and reflection.

Speaking from a personal appropriation of God love for me, I can say that if God creates me and continues to create me through my own personality, temperaments, family history, material possessions, intellectual capabilities, spiritual gifts, countless acts of goodness of others, and even through my own brokenness, then I am who I am because of all of these things that have become parts of my life. Upon reflection, I realize that, on the one hand, God creates me because he loves me personally, and God does so precisely in and through the things that I have received in my life. On the other hand, if God's love for me has been manifested in the things I have received, then is not that what I can and ought to offer back to God in the service of others? For gifts are meant to be shared. The moment I stop sharing my gifts with others I also cease being created by God. God's act of creation is an ongoing act, and it is in cooperating with God's gifts and in using those gifts in the service of others that I continue to be created. Hence, the mode of giving becomes the mode of receiving. From Grace is received abundant grace. That is what the Mystery of Love has revealed to those who have faith in the good and living God.

This line of thought needs to be explained further from the point of view of Lonergan's *Transcendent Love* that we have discussed. We have seen how human knowing progresses in four interrelated levels: experience, understanding, judging and acting. All these levels can be attained by mere

---

35. See Dunne, *Lonergan and Spirituality*, 1–54. I also want to refer the reader to Lonergan's *Method in Theology* for further exploration of his levels of human knowing.

human capability. In Lonergan's method, there is another level of knowing; it is the highest level which Lonergan calls "love." It is the *Transcendent Love* we have discussed. This is the love that is revealed to us by God. It comes to us, or rather is born in us, as a result of an act of religious faith in a good and loving God, whereby faith is defined as "a judgment of value born of religious love."[36] It is this love that generates faith, hope and charity, the three theological virtues that make it possible for our actions to be the actions that reflect and cooperate with the creating actions of divine love. In the first four levels of love we are encouraged to be *attentive, intelligent, reasonable* and *responsible* in regards to our experience, understanding, judging and acting. But in this fifth level we are called to be *in love* with God and thus in love with all of God's creation. It is in this sense of being *in love* that we can perceive everything as gifts from God for the purpose of the ongoing creation of the world.

Lonergan's understanding of the fifth level of human knowing as "being *in love* with God" can be useful to our discussion on the Ignatian "Contemplation to Attain Love." The whole purpose of the exercise on the "Contemplation to Attain Love" is clearly "union with God in action," commonly known as "contemplation in action." To better understand the meaning of the Ignatian Contemplation to Attain Love, which is the final exercise of the entire *Spiritual Exercises* of Saint Ignatius, it will help to briefly survey the key movements in the *Spiritual Exercises*, and then to explore how they connect to contribute to the Contemplation to Attain Love and various movements of the *Spiritual Exercises*.

The *Spiritual Exercises* of Saint Ignatius spreading through the thirty days comprise of four main movements, known as the "four weeks." Ignatius structures the entire *Spiritual Exercises* with the goal of divine union, perceived as a dynamic state of life in cooperation with God's ongoing creation. In order to attain this noble goal, Ignatius first presents the Principle and Foundation, the first and most foundational consideration of the entire *Spiritual Exercises*. In it, he defines the destiny of human beings, that they are created to know, to love and to serve God; in doing so, they save their own souls and the souls of those with whom they serve. In order to do so effectively, Ignatius recommends that human beings must attain an attitude of healthy balance toward created things. In his view, everything that human beings have attained for themselves: material possessions and spiritual gifts are for them to use in order to know, to love, and to serve God in knowing, loving and serving others. Ignatius even considers life circumstances, such as good health and sickness, wealth and poverty, even social status

---

36. Dunne, *Lonergan and Spirituality*, 118.

and misfortune, as the means to attain union with God. Consequently, if these things—be they possessions, states of life or life circumstances—hinder rather help human beings to attain their destiny, they ought to let go of them (SpEx 23).

The Principle and Foundation, as described, builds the foundation on which the entire *Spiritual Exercises* are based. The purpose of the *Spiritual Exercises* are twofold: 1) To help the retreatant (one who make the *Spiritual Exercises* in the context of a retreat) to be aware of his or her disordered attachments so as to counter them with virtues, and 2) to discover God's individual will for him or her, which implies an attempt to discover a way of life in the trajectory toward knowing, loving and serving God by knowing, loving and serving others.

Immediately following the Principle and Foundation, Ignatius discusses the method for the Examination of Consciousness and he presents it as an effective way to reflect so as to discern the direction of one's spirit on a daily basis. In the discernment of spirits, it is crucial that one pay attention to the movement within one's heart, for example, joyful or sad, motivated or bored, patient or impatient, anxious or peaceful, etc. One needs to trace the source of the movement one feels and to direct it to a fruitful end. The Examination of Consciousness teaches us to discern the various spirits from within by guiding us through five concrete steps: 1) To give thanks to God for what I have received, 2) to ask God for the grace to know any sinful tendency, 3) to examine my day moment by moment in order to know where my spirit may have been and whether or not it is in tune with God or has gone in the opposite direction, 4) to ask God for forgiveness, and 5) to beg for the grace to be able to resolve my life for the better (SpEx 43). Ignatius instructs that the Examination of Consciousness should be about fifteen minutes and carried out twice a day, at noon and in the evening, or at least once at the end of the day when one looks back on the whole day and examine one's spiritual movements applying the five steps described above.

Both the Principle and Foundation and the Examination of Consciousness are introduced at the beginning of the retreat to prepare the retreatant for the actual contemplations in the four weeks of the *Spiritual Exercises*. In the first week of the *Spiritual Exercises*, Ignatius presents and explains the nature of sin and how sins disrupt the flow of God's grace and thus prevent human beings from attaining their destiny. Ignatius does not simply present the personal sins that one has committed. That has already been done when the retreatant was guided by the director in making the General Examination of Consciousness which was followed by the General Confession of his or her personal sins. Ignatius's aim in the first week is to help the retreatant to deepen his or her knowledge of sin by guiding him or her to explore the history of sins. For this reason, Ignatius presents to the retreatant the sins of fallen angels and the sins of Adam and Eve (SpEx 45–54), which he invites the retreatant to consider in their prayer. With the use of the senses and imagination, the retreatant contemplates the nature of the sins and their destructive impact on human lives. Only after the retreatant has considered the sins of fallen angels and of Adam and Eve does Ignatius discuss personal sins (SpEx 55–61). Ignatius presents the exercises on sin in this order to underscore that personal sins have a history, and that history intertwines with the history of the sin of all spiritual creatures, beginning with the fallen angels, through Adam and Eve and down to the present day.

Theologically, this is an important step in understanding God's creation and salvation. Many people think of sins only as private and personal. They do not realize that sins have a social and cultural context and dynamic. It is important to note that in acknowledging the nature and impact of social sins, we do not imply that society and culture can sin. Rather, we are exposing the seriousness and damage personal sins can do to others in a given society and thus can obstruct the moral integrity of that society and culture.

Personal sins and social sins condition each other. The two types of sin are reciprocal. In our contemporary context, many people can be passionate about social justice issues such as discrimination against others because of their race, ethnicity or gender; intolerance toward people of different faith traditions; indifference to political refugees, etc. From the Christian perspective, these are manifestations of social sins. But to work against these social sins so as to promote a more tolerant and peaceful world, one must know what justice is from the biblical foundation and how it has developed in the teaching of the Church. In doing so, one cultivates in himself a sense of justice that is not merely based on fairness, but on the love and compassion of God who always protects the innocent, cares for the neglected and frees the oppressed. A just soul contributes to the wellbeing of the society and makes it just. One cannot effectively work for social justice unless one's soul is ordered. If the person's soul is disordered, how does he imagine himself working for justice? His view on justice has already been distorted by the disorder of his soul. He must work hard to cultivate virtues for himself first before he can hope to bring about a just society.

Sometimes one can be deceived into thinking that one's main duty as a citizen is to fight for the rights of others so as to bring about a just society. Such a person can be passionate about social justice issues and even prone to anger and resentment when her agenda for social justice is not acknowledged and put forth by others. The truth, however, is that most of the issues may in fact arise from within her disordered soul. The quest for human progress must be a personal quest, and a disordered soul cannot achieve an authentic and personal quest. To the extent that a just society does not exist, it is because there has not been a just soul. Thus, in the words of Tad Dunne we assert that "we can trace the outer breakdown of social order to some inner breakdown in the personal order, just as we can trace social progress to its sources in an inner personal achievement of the soul."[37]

The *Spiritual Exercises* of Saint Ignatius are meant for individual persons who strive to find the meaning and purpose of their lives by discovering God's will for them. Ignatius deeply believes that salvation is personal. God's salvation must take place in the individual person because God creates each of us personally and thus God also redeems us personally. But God desires to save all, and so, my salvation, though personal as it is understood, cannot be separated from that of others and of the whole of God's creation. It is from this social dynamic of sin and salvation that we can establish the interconnection between personal and social sins and salvation. Just as personal sins are conditioned by the cultural and social sins, so too, personal redemption is conditioned by the redemption of other people. Ignatius is very keen on the relationship between the personal and social sins. He presents the history of sins in the first week in order to underscore their interconnectedness, so that the whole aim of the entire *Spiritual Exercises* may become clear: In contemplating the nature and impact of sin, the retreatant comes to realize the need for his or her personal salvation as well as desire to follow Christ in the world to fight against the sin of injustice that has become endemic. But spiritual progress always needs to be effected at the personal level and then moved out to the social dynamic. At the end of the first week of the *Spiritual Exercises*, the retreatant comes to a realization that not only she is forgiven and loved by God, but more importantly, she feels inspired to know, love and serve God in Jesus Christ, the Incarnation of God.

The objective of the second week of the *Spiritual Exercises* can be perceived as the natural outcome of the first week. The retreatant's question at the end of the first week was, "How should I follow Jesus Christ in the world?" In the second week Ignatius helps the retreatant to explore the answer to the question by presenting the two contrasting Standards of life. The Standard of Satan, the Prince of Demons, immediately attracts people because it promises riches and honor as the ground for pride. But Ignatius points out the snare of this standard of life: it allures people with empty promises that often lead them to spiritual dryness and even depression. Then Ignatius presents another Standard of life, one featured from Jesus Christ, the King of the Universe, who disdains the standard of life mooted by Satan. In contrast to Satan, Jesus presents a vision of life in solidarity

37. Dunne, *Lonergan and Spirituality*, 1.

and interdependence, which could in fact result in poverty and contempt. Christ's Standard does not immediately attract people like that of Satan; rather it is presented as an alternative to Satan's. After presenting the two standards of life, Ignatius does the same thing as in the first week: He invites the retreatant to utilize his or her senses, imagination and intellect to consider and pray for an understanding of the contrasting truths in the two value systems, and to resolve to follow the value system presented by Jesus Christ. It is evident that those who choose the Standard of Christ will face the challenges from the opposing Standard, and thus they will be put to a test.

The third week of the *Spiritual Exercises* helps deepen the retreatant's choice to follow Christ by guiding him or her to consider the possible consequences of the choice. The retreatant is invited to contemplate the suffering Christ in his passion and death on the Cross and to imagine how his suffering exists today in those who are suffering because of sickness, war, broken relationship, marginalization, abandonment and abuse. One feels the suffering of Christ in the sufferings of the world and is moved to help alleviate suffering.

But suffering is not a final answer. In the end all suffering must be transformed into compassion. In the fourth and final week of the *Spiritual Exercises*, Ignatius invites the retreatant to contemplate the resurrection of Jesus. The event of Jesus's resurrection cannot be scientifically proven, because the disciples of Jesus did not see him raised from the tomb and rising to life. Rather, after his resurrection, Jesus revealed the mystery of his life, death and resurrection to the disciples in a series of apparitions he appeared to them, conversed with them, ate with them, and reminded them of who he was. In doing so, he affirmed their belief in him as the Risen One; thus they were able to receive his Spirit and be strengthened. Consequently they went forward spreading the Good News about him with joy. Such is the story of the Christian faith.

Seen from this perspective, the joy of the resurrection of Jesus cannot be interpreted apart from his life, suffering and death. The disciples could not recognize the Resurrected Christ until he revealed the truth about him as he interpreted to them how scripture had talked about him. In doing so, he affirmed them in their mission. Their joy in his resurrection must be interpreted from the whole trajectory of his life, particularly his suffering and death. The Easter joy experienced by the disciples enables them to witness to a new way of life modeled by Jesus where unity, love, compassion and solidarity are present. This new way of life originates in the standard of life of Jesus presented in the second week of the *Spiritual Exercises* as an alternative to a way of life contrasting to the Standard of Satan which often results in narcissism, division, hatred and lack of peace.

It is in this dynamic of the four weeks of the *Spiritual Exercises* that we interpret the Ignatian Contemplation to Attain Love. As I mentioned earlier, for Ignatius love has to be manifest in deeds more than in words. Now, in the context of the entire *Spiritual Exercises*, above all in the contemplation of the Resurrected Christ, the word "deeds" acquires a theological meaning. Ignatius is not suggesting that all of our love for God and for others ought to be measured by our deeds. But he is implying that we can find God in what we do as much as we can feel God's presence in our prayer. Ignatian spirituality really puts an emphasis on the discerning and carrying out God's will in the world in the following of Jesus Christ. We could say that for Ignatius, prayer alone is not sufficient. Ignatius believes that God's work of creation is an ongoing work; and by cooperating with God's grace in laboring with God we bring about God's dream for the world. But how distinct is our work in comparison to other kinds of work, and how do we measure our success in the work that we do?

To answer these questions, let us refer to Ignatius's final points in the *Spiritual Exercises* (SpEx 234–37); these points together characterize the Ignatian "Contemplation in Action."

First, Ignatius asks the retreatant to reflect on the truth that all the things he or she has received up to that point in life are gifts from God: My family, religious background, education, friends, co-workers, material possessions and spiritual talents are all God's gifts for me so that I may continue using them for the glory of God in the service of others. I might or might not have recognized these things as pure gifts. But there is a distinction between what I know now and what I did not know before: I now am able to feel and savor these things as gifts, as opposed to seeing them as my own creation or acknowledging them as gifts from others without a deep sense of gratitude for God. This felt sense of God's love, which I have appropriated in the gifts He has bestowed on me, moves me to offer all back to God in the service of others.

Second, not only does God bestow on me abundant gifts, but God is present in creation now to sustain them in life: sun, moon, stars and other celestial realities continue operating in their intelligent way; inanimate objects, plants, animals and human beings are living and being sustained in life by God; but each does so in its own intelligent operation. I can now marvel at God's creatures and feel God's presence in them. I suddenly sense that the world is charged with the grandeur of God, as Gerald Manley Hopkins the poet put it. I am moved with gratitude for God who continues to sustain me in and through creation.

Third, God is at work in the world. As much as I feel God's presence in the world, I also have a sense that many people do not experience God's presence. And so God continues working and making Himself present. God's creation is not yet complete. I experience a paradox: There is a sense that God is "already present" in all of God's creation; but at the same time, there is so much suffering in the world: War, division, intolerance and abuse of God's creation still exist. God's creation is not complete; the work is on, and I feel the call to participate in God's progress of creation.

Finally, once again Ignatius invites the retreatant to contemplate God's grace in realizing the truth that even the capacity to experience God in the way he or she just has, it is bestowed by God. In the end, the retreatant comes to a realization that all indeed is a gift from God. So he or she concludes the prayer period, giving praise and thanks to God in the words of the Our Father.

As we can see then, the well-known characteristic of Ignatian spirituality, being "contemplative in action," is to be interpreted from the "Contemplation to Attain Love," presented by Ignatius as the final contemplation of the *Spiritual Exercises*. In it we see how Ignatius understands Divine Union as a union of divine love and human response to that love in a life of grace, so that everything a person does becomes an embodiment of God's presence in the world. This type of Divine Union becomes possible when a person correctly appropriates the destiny of human beings as explained in the Principle and Foundation, deepens it in the experience of God's love for him or her despite his or her sins in the first week, envisions the value system of Jesus Christ, the Incarnation of God in the choice made in the second week, tests it against the challenge to stand up for and witness to that value system of Christ in the third week, and fully incorporates it in a life in union with God in action in the fourth week.

Conclusion

SAINT AUGUSTINE, IN HIS *Confessions*, wrote something unforgettable: "You have created us for yourself, O God, and our heart is restless until it rests in you." Throughout the centuries of Christianity, these words of Augustine have been referred to as the classic teaching about the human desire for the transcendent, a desire that cannot find satisfaction in the material but only in the Spirit of God existing as its own source.

The consumerist society in which we live at such a fast pace seems to offer a contrasting experience. We have advanced much in science and technology, but scientific discoveries demand and rely on empirical evidence without resort to a need for the spiritual realm. The reason is quite simple: things belonging to the spiritual realm cannot be perceived by physical eyes or measured tangibly. Science rules out the existence of a spiritual realm by its own methodology. The demand for empirical evidence has instilled in us the unfortunate habit of understanding reality only at the level of appearance; thus we limit our capacity for knowledge to the material world. It is no surprise that we have such a hard time awakening to the spiritual realm.

Furthermore, we live in a digital age whereby true reality can be replaced by a visual reality we have created for ourselves. Video games become the means for self-gratification. Instead of utilizing new technological inventions such as online video (you-tube), text-messages and other online means for better communication, we misuse these means when we become addicted to them. Similar to scientific inventions and discoveries, visual reality can provide immediate gratification and give someone a false sense of satisfaction. One can isolate oneself by spending many hours playing video games online or constantly texting and calling friends or family members while he or she should focus on the task at hand. The result is alarming: Fatigue, lack of focus and confusion after many hours locking oneself in front of a computer screen or on a cellphone. The reason is quite simple: the human brain has adjusted itself to a new condition that must constantly take in information; under this new condition, the brain dictates the person's behavior, and thus, he or she is controlled by the distorted and unbalanced brain.

We must rescue ourselves from this havoc by cultivating a more healthy way of life where the mind can regain its most noble function. The human mind should not be treated like a machine. The mind needs time to rest, reflect and process the information received through the senses. All human knowledge must begin with the senses; but meaningful knowledge must end in the intellect. Without the mind's capacity to reflect and to evaluate the information received by the senses, there can be no intellectual knowledge but only fragmentation of information. We must do what we can to sustain the mind's capacity for reflection, which in turn, enables it to make value judgments on things; otherwise we run the risk of becoming like a machine, operating on a set of conditions that we do not have control over.

Many people who are aware of the diminishing and possible loss of our human capacity for the spiritual reality have looked for ways to cope the hectic of our life through yoga practice and other Buddhist meditative methods. Zen meditation is what comes to mine at the moment. "Zen" refers to the practice in which the practitioners sit in meditation for hours on end. In the lotus position, for example, a Buddhist practitioner sits with eyes closed, focusing on the breaths he or she is taking. An outside observer may have a tendency to dismiss such a practice as useless and wasteful. But imagine the degree of focus and the amount of energy a practitioner must put into this type of meditation. Many people who practice Zen have found that the most difficult thing in meditation is to control one's flow of thoughts. Buddhist practitioners have provided valuable insights into how to control one's thoughts in meditation. They know that the first step in the discovery of the true self comes from the awareness of one's own breath. Through the breathing-in and breathing-out, one begins to be aware of his or her own existence and thus is able to bring the thoughts from the mind down to the heart and harmonize his or her thoughts with the rhythms of the breath.

This is exactly how Christian contemplation should begin. As we have seen in our discussion on the *Jesus Prayer* how strenuously the contemplative must put in the effort to bring his or her mind into the heart through the rhythm of his or her breathing. Seen from this perspective, both Buddhist meditation and Christian contemplation are techniques that can counterbalance the effects of the digital age, fast-paced and consumerist society in which we live that has weakened the human capacity to focus on the present task, which results in the mind's diminishing capacity for reflection.

The topic discussed in this book was Christian contemplation, not on Buddhist meditative methods. However, the question can be raised: Why is it that many people today, Christians included, find Buddhist meditation an attractive and effective way to cope with the hectic reality of their lives? The answers to this question will help to underscore the distinctive characteristics of Christian contemplation.

There is a difference between Christian contemplation and Buddhist meditation. The Buddha, the Founder of Buddhism, did not come to realize his need to sit in meditation until he had been awakened to the truth of the suffering of the world. Buddha's father confined him to the royal palace without any contact to the outside world. In doing so, his father had hoped that he would be content with what he saw inside the palace. But once the Buddha managed to escape the royal palace and discovered for himself the truth about the world outside the royal way of life, he found himself confronted with a new reality contrary to what he had seen. He realized that the life inside the royal palace was constructed to cover up the reality of suffering and keep him ignorant of it. Thus Buddha gained the first insight into the spiritual life: *There is an illusion, or a falsely constructed meaning that we often mistake for the true meaning of life; through meditation one can become free of this constructed reality and thus see reality for what it is.* Zen meditation aims to remove all misconceptions about reality so that one can perceive reality for what it is.

The second insight we learn from Zen Buddhism is that *in Zen it is believed that the essence of things can be attained through a non-attaining state of mind*. This understanding is based on the principle of non-duality which asserts that things do not exist as opposites and do not cancel out each other. For example, black and white, beauty and ugliness, good and bad are not in opposition to each other; rather they are indestructible truths about reality. Our mind perceives these indestructible truths as opposites because our knowledge of them has been conditioned by our sensation, perception, thought, and consciousness which are constructed meanings. Zen practitioners do not deny constructed meanings, but they distinguish between these meanings, which comprise *conventional reality*, from true knowledge attained by the enlightened mind that can grasp the essence of *absolute reality*. The indestructible truth of things cannot be attained by means of empirical evidence and human reason alone, because the latter produce only conventional reality, whereas indestructible truth of things can only come as a result of the mind's comprehension of the essence of things. Zen Buddhist meditation aims to remove all constructed meanings so as to attain the state of pure *emptiness*, known as the non-attaining state of mind, whereby the emptiness itself opens up the possibility for the mind to perceive things for what they truly are. Thus, the saying "all forms are empty and all emptiness is form" makes sense from the point of view of the principle of non-duality.

In Christianity, there is a difference. Christian contemplation, as we have seen, begins with God and ends in God. In other words, Christian contemplation has but one purpose: Divine Union. Similar to Buddhist meditation, the first aim in Christian contemplation is the removal of disordered attachments and cultivation of virtues. That is why a Christian in contemplation, must cultivate an attitude of *detachment* to the things that prevent him or her from union with God, be they material goods, mental states, or life circumstances. Similar to the concept of *emptiness* in Zen Buddhism, Christian detachment serves as the means to the end. In other words, just as the *Buddhist emptiness* opens up the possibility for the mind to apprehend reality in its pure essence, so too, the *Christian detachment* enables the Christian contemplative to be free of his or her disordered love for created things and to love them only in God. Seen from the perspective of *self-emptying*, both Buddhist meditation and Christian contemplation aim at the removal of all illusions attached to the self so as to attain the true self capable of perceiving reality from the transcendent perspective. But *Christian self-emptying is an emptying in love of God first and foremost, and then and only then can it transform the love of self and others in God; whereas the Buddhist emptiness is an emptiness of the false self so as to attain the true self without a need to reference to a Creator God.*

Furthermore, in Christianity, Jesus Christ is believed to be God in the flesh (John 1:14), so the Christian contemplative unites himself with Christ and takes on the identity of Christ. But this divine identity which the Christian contemplative takes on has already been achieved in the resurrected Christ himself as "the first fruits" of the living. Jesus Christ offers himself completely to the will of God to the point of death on the Cross, because that is the way he can completely empty his divine spirit into the human spirit, which in turn, transforms his human spirit into the divine. Christ's death reveals the ultimate power of the human spirit when it is united with the divine spirit. In this sense, Christ's death satisfies God's intention and purpose for humanity, and as a result, God raises him up to life eternal. Christ's humanity is transformed into the divine reality without losing its human identity. Because of what Christ has accomplished through his death, a death in obedience to God, which is also a death in conformity with the depth of his own human spirit, the unity between his two natures was possible in his person. In this sense, Christ's death and resurrection, taken together, opens up the possibility for a contemplative to a new way of life in union with God in him.

Thus we see that The Logic of the Incarnation informs the Christian understanding of contemplation. Just as in the Incarnation, God has *emptied* himself of the divine nature in order to become human (Philippians

2:6–8), so too, only when human beings *empty* themselves of the things that prevent them from becoming like God can they be united with the divine. Christian contemplation follows the same pattern of the contemplative Christ. This pattern, however, should not be understood as a mere imitation of Christ. Rather, the ultimate aim of Christian contemplation is union with God in Christ. To imitate Christ requires that one observe Christ's way of life as it is recorded in the Gospel and make it relevant and applicable in one's own way of life; whereas, a life in union with Christ enables one to live with an identity of Christ in the world. One can imitate Christ without an experience of divine union with Christ; whereas once a divine union is felt in one's heart, one cannot but live as Christ lives in him or her. As Saint Paul says, "It is no longer I who live, but it is Christ who lives in me" (Galatians 2:20). In this sense, the life in union with Christ comprises a higher degree of perfection than that of a mere imitation of him.

It must be reemphasized that divine union is a state of life in grace. A Christian contemplative's capacity to recognize his or her sinfulness, which is the fundamental condition for union with God, is itself a divine gift. Sin consists of both personal and communal dimensions, because sin is, by nature, relational. One's sins always offend God, self and others. A person cannot fathom the damage his sins have caused to himself and to others unless he recognizes first that life is created to be good and holy. A person's sins not only destroy the image of God in which he has been created, but his sins also destroy the image of God in others, whose lives have been negatively impacted. In the language of Saint Paul, to be a Christian means to become a member of the Body of Christ (1 Cor 12:27), and as members of the same Body, all Christians are connected to each other and ultimately connected to Christ the head of the Body. From this point of view, one's sins are personal, but they are at the same time communal; the two dimensions of sin are reciprocal.

Christian salvation, therefore, should be interpreted from two relational dimensions: personal and communal. Through contemplation, a contemplative knows herself as a sinner in need of God's mercy. But at the same time, she realizes that she is a sinner but loved by God and has been redeemed by Christ. Hence, the contemplative comes to contemplation with a humble heart like that of the tax-collector who prays to God beating his breast and asks for forgiveness, saying, "God have mercy on me a sinner" (Luke 18:13). A tax collector was indeed considered a sinner in first century Palestinian religious context. But it is precisely in his realization of his sinfulness that he becomes humble. It is important to note that the tax-collector's humility does not merely consist of his realization and acceptance of his lower status in comparison to the Pharisee. Rather, his is a *religious humility* that originates from the heart of a sinner in need of God's love. Unlike a common understanding of humility as an acceptance of one's moderate and less important place in comparison to others, religious humility comprises an essential part of the tax-collector's religious identity. He becomes humble before God, and in his humbleness, the tax-collector realizes his identity as a sinner yet loved by God.

We observe a similar theme of *religious humility* in Zen Buddhism and from Rudolf Steiner's discussion on humility as the most fundamental attitude in the spiritual life. We have seen how the Pharisee craves for superiority over the tax-collector. From a Buddhist point of view, the Pharisee could be perceived as feeling the need to be superior to the tax-collector; this in turn, would have clouded his own judgment about the tax-collector as well as about himself. From Steiner's view of higher knowledge, we can assert that the Pharisee has not cultivated the sense of reverence and respect for the tax-collector that he should have, and this lack of reverence and respect, in turn, stirs in him an urge to judge the tax-collector to be someone with a lower status than himself. In Steiner's analysis, this very urge to pass judgment on others obstructs the spiritual view of soul, as we pointed out. From the Christian point of view, however, one cannot base one's evaluation of the Pharisee's attitude merely on his view about himself in relation to the tax-collector; one must perceive the Pharisee's judgment of the tax-collector from his relationship, or lack thereof, with God. The Pharisee's judgment of the tax-collector implies a different image of God than the God of love in whom the tax-collector has believed. In other words, the Pharisee has mistaken the true God of love for a judgmental God. Further, he projects that image on God onto the tax-collector, and this fundamentally goes against the foundation of the Christian faith. Christian contemplation, as we discussed, must be grounded on the image of a good and loving God, not a harsh and judgmental God.

Another insight gained from the discussions in this pertains to the meaning of suffering. From the Christian perspective, *suffering is not good in and of itself, but without the experience of suffering caused by the letting go of an insatiable desire for material comfort and preconception, one's spiritual life cannot flourish.*

Everyone knows that making choices is not easy. To have to choose one thing over another oftentimes reveals one's internal conflicts, especially when one has to make a choice between two alternatives that appear equally good. In the spiritual life, the conflicts arising from two or more alternatives become more vivid when one must let go of the things that have been conceived as helpful but in truth obstruct one's spiritual growth. Jesus says, "Unless a grain of wheat falls into the earth and dies, it remains just a single grain; but if it dies, it bears much fruit" (John 12:24). Not being able to let go of disordered attachments to things or people would be like a grain of wheat that remains a grain. But a person who detaches himself from the things that are not useful to spiritual growth is like letting a grain of wheat fall into the earth, take roots and grow and thus produce fruit. The analogy applies universally, across cultural and religious traditions. The reason for the universal application lies in the fact that every human person possesses a free will. The human will is the intellectual capability to choose what is good and fulfilling. But when the will is confronted with conflicting desires, it no longer functions as it should, because in this case the intellect itself becomes clouded with incorrect knowledge of reality; thus its value judgments do not correlate with reality. The will is presented with conflicting desires and thus suffers as a consequence. Contemplation aims to enlighten the intellect to its principal function, which is its capacity to distinguish between the good and the bad. Once the mind is able to elucidate the difference between the two alternatives, then the will can choose that which is good and avoid the bad.

The concept of *suffering* needs to be broadened to include not only the suffering caused in the letting go of material comfort when the very comfort itself prevents one from growing spiritually, but it should also include the suffering caused in letting go of one's preconceptions. The story of the Pharisee who desires superiority over the tax-collector can be used again to demonstrate this point. From the Buddhist perspective, the Pharisee's craving for superiority produces his own suffering, which originates in his ignorance. He has been deceived into thinking that his life is worth more than the life of the tax-collector.

Buddhist meditation aims to enlighten the mind to the truth that can dispel all deceptions caused by incorrect preconception. The wisdom inherited in the Buddhist principle of the *Middle Way* teaches that all things ought to be kept in moderation so as to avoid extremes as much as possible. The Middle Way does not imply a sense of balance as on a scale where both sides must maintain an equal weight. Rather it is a middle way between one may need to be more courageous at one time than another, or to choose a different career path now than the previous one. The criteria for choosing the Middle Way are based on a knowledge of one's own characteristic traits, temperament and talents, and the best judgment based on these in a given context. It is in grasping this teaching and putting it into practice that ignorance can be uprooted and thus the suffering caused by ignorance can be alleviated and even eliminated altogether.

In Christian contemplation, *detachment and sacrifice* are perceived as the two sides of the same reality of the spiritual life; without one or the other, the spiritual life cannot flourish. The suffering caused by the sacrifice made in detachment can be transformed by the divine grace which guides the person's effort to discern a path of life that leads to union with God and to fight against the temptation toward sin and destruction.

Let us compare for a moment *Christian discernment* to the Buddhist *Middle Way*. We have seen how the rules for the *discernment of spirits* in the *Spiritual Exercises* of Saint Ignatius of Loyola present a method for discerning a pathway that leads to life in union with God. From this set of rules Ignatius describes *spiritual consolation* as a movement toward God that often generates faith, hope and love; whereas, *spiritual desolation* is a contrary movement: a movement away from God that often triggers negative emotions such as lack of joy and disturbance of peace which result in lack of faith, hope and love. As a general rule, Ignatius teaches that in time of desolation, one should not make any new decision nor change the decision that has already been made in time of consolation (SpEx 318). Rather one should be patient with oneself, pray to God for the deliverance from distress, and counter desolation by seeking out help from others. Furthermore, Ignatius teaches that there are causes to spiritual desolation. The first cause has to do with one's own laziness and negligence in the spiritual life; i.e., one has not striven to cultivate the discipline needed to establish and nurture an appropriate spiritual life. The second cause can be permitted by God as a way to test one's spiritual growth and humility. In regard to the second cause Ignatius says that sometimes God permits the person to experience spiritual desolation so that he or she realizes that it is not his or her own effort alone that produces spiritual consolation, but ultimately it is God's grace that satisfies his or her soul with deep spiritual joy.

There is no doubt that a contemplative suffers in time of spiritual desolation, especially when the desolation prolongs. To further explore the theme of spiritual desolation in spiritual life and the suffering entailed in it, we turned to Teresa of Avila's *Interior Castle*. We have seen how Teresa describes the seven dwelling places in her work and identifies the sixth dwelling place as the most difficult stage in the soul's journey to union with God. Teresa shares a similar view to that of Ignatius. She says that during the sixth stage the soul is engaged to the Lord Jesus Christ as in a betrothal. During this period of betrothal, Christ is testing the soul's loyalty to him. The soul has gone through the first five stages in prayer and has arrived at the beginning of union with Christ. But now the soul desires a deeper love for Christ and is ready for further growth in intimacy with Christ. Christ, however, withdraws his presence from the soul for the moment in order to test her faithfulness. As a result, the soul keeps desiring Christ in his absence. It is in the continuing desire for Christ that suffering of the soul occurs.

We can observe here a different perspective from the Buddhist view on suffering. In Buddhist spirituality, sufferings are believed to be caused by constructed meanings. The reason is that when the constructed meanings (or preconceptions) do not correlate with reality as one has expected, then one experiences conflicts within oneself, and conflicts in turn result in suffering. Once constructed meanings are removed by the enlightened mind as a result of meditation, then suffering disappears.

In Christian spirituality, the cause of suffering does not originate in mere preconceptions and prejudices, though no doubt these comprise part of the cause of suffering. Rather, in a mystical sense of the word, *suffering can be caused by God as a way to teach the soul to grow in relationship with the divine.* In the case of Teresa of Avila for example, the suffering of her soul is caused by her desire for union with Christ. It is not just the soul that endures suffering while feeling of God's absence, but God also suffers as a result of the distance between the soul and God, which is so close to God and yet still not completely united. It is in this sense that suffering can be transformed into love, for love is both the cause and the fulfillment of the heart's desire for union. It is from this perspective that one can understand Teresa's suffering, which she described as the feeling of "being abandoned by God." In other words, Teresa hopes in God's providence even in time when her soul feels distanced from God. In such a time, Teresa understands that the soul is being stretched by God which causes her to suffer, and she accepts the suffering and describes it as a *wound of love*, a wound that teaches her to love God for God's sake and not for her own spiritual gratification.

In one of the rules regarding spiritual desolation, Ignatius states that sometimes God allows the person to experience desolation so that she learns to stretch her love, service and praise of God without expecting consolation and increased graces in return (SpEx 322). Both Teresa of Avila and Ignatius of Loyola value spiritual suffering as a condition for spiritual growth. However, one should not take this value judgment to imply that suffering is good in and of itself. Without the capacity to be transformed into love, suffering has no meaning. Further, one must be cautious not to assume that everyone is called to or capable of enduring suffering in the same way and to the same degree. Teresa herself observed that most of the religious sisters in her community reached the fifth dwelling place in their spiritual journey, but very few could pass to the sixth dwelling place. The aim, however, is not to avoid suffering at all costs, but to create possibilities for a more balanced life, so that when suffering does occur in one's spiritual journey, which is inevitable, one will be ready to endure it with a more generous heart.

The final insight gained from the discussions in this book can be summarized as follows: *One's spiritual practices and the insights gained from them are not meant for one's own enjoyment; rather, spiritual practices aim to help alleviate the suffering of others.* The final stage in the spiritual life ought not to be a static state, but ought to be a dynamic state of life where the contemplative person naturally moves to love and care for others.

We have seen how Rudolf Steiner underscores the need for engagement in the betterment of others as part of one's attempt to cultivate spiritual knowledge. For Steiner, no spiritual practices will benefit one's spiritual progress if their purpose consists only in self-betterment. In other words, the capacity for veneration of created reality which one has successfully cultivated through spiritual practice and the degree of humility one has achieved through spiritual discipline become useless if they do not enlighten the minds of others and help alleviate their suffering. Self-enjoyment is the enemy of the spiritual life. Steiner observes that the fulfillment of one's spiritual goal depends on one's desire and ability to make available one's insights and practices to the betterment of others. If this condition is not fulfilled, the opposite result will be true: Instead of fulfilling one's destiny, the very spiritual insights one gained and spiritual practices one undertook can obstruct one's spiritual progress and even destroy one's spiritual life in the end.

Buddhist spirituality shares this conviction. Once a Buddhist practitioner has achieved the state of *nirvana* (an awakening state of mind that eliminates all sufferings caused by ignorance), he or she does not cease to practice meditation. Rather, the person who has achieved enlightenment (called a "bodhisattva") naturally moves to help other *sentient beings* (beings that can feel pain and suffering in their bodies) to ease their suffering. From this point of view, *nirvana* and *compassion* for other sentient beings are two inseparable aspects of the Buddha nature. This view is often illustrated in an image of a human face with two eyes, each eye represents an aspect of the awakening state, and both eyes reflect the one and only face. Thus, one observes that deep in the teaching of the Buddha lies an understanding of what can be described as an *active nirvana*, a nirvana that is not a standing still (inactive) state of life. Rather, it is an active nirvana in the sense of giving care to other sentient beings. The term *bodhisattva*: the Buddha, the Enlightened One, in an ultimate sense denotes someone who meditates not only for his or her own sake but also for the sake of all sentient beings.

In Christian spiritual practice, there is an essential difference in contrast to Steiner's and the Buddhist view. Jesus's teaching on the love of God and the love of neighbor can be observed from the Double Commandment where it is said that one should love God with all one's heart, with all one's mind, with all one's strength; and one should love one's neighbor as one's self (Luke 10:27). The two loves are not separated. Jesus reiterates the teaching in the Gospel according to Matthew when he says, "Truly I tell you, just as you did it to one of the least of these who are members of my family, you did it to me" (Matt 25:40). This saying implies that to the extent one does not offer love and care to another human being in need, one does not love and serve God in the neighbor (Matt 25:45).

But note how one's love for God is without measure, as can be seen in the phrase, "One should love God with all one's heart, with all one's mind, and with all one's strength." Clearly the love of God and the love of others are not the same. Jesus did not say that one should love one's neighbor above all things. Only one's love for God is absolute; that is, one should love God with all of one's being. The love one has for another originates from one's love for God and is measured from one's authentic love of one's self.

Christian contemplation aims at divine union, as we have said, and this union is a union of love. So in an ultimate sense, divine union is made manifest in the divine love suffusing the heart of the contemplative who, in turns, is able to love God with all of her being and love others with the same love she has felt from God. This is why Saint John says, "We love because He has loved us first" (1 John 4:19). The contemplative mediates God's love to others. But it is not so much she who does it; rather, it is Christ's spirit who gives love to others through her. Saint Paul must have felt such a divine love in him when he uttered the words, "It is no longer I who live, but it is Christ who lives in me (Gal 2:20).

In the third week of the *Spiritual Exercises* Ignatius of Loyola guides the contemplative to contemplate the suffering Christ in his passion and death on the Cross and to imagine how his suffering exists today in those who are suffering because of sickness, war, broken relationship, marginalization, abandonment and abuse. The Ignatian understanding of Christ's suffering and death goes beyond a mere emotional stage. One does not stop short at a feeling of sorrow for Christ's suffering and death, but one is moved to contemplate the suffering of those who are mistreated, marginalized, and abused in the world today. All human beings, and indeed all of God's creation, deserve respect, protection and prevention from all forms of violation of their given dignity, because they are created for life and are meant for the Mystical Body of Christ. To ignore the suffering of others means to ignore the ongoing suffering of Christ's Body. Christian contemplation awakens a Christian contemplative to this existential reality of suffering and to alleviate it as much as possible. Seen from this perspective, Christian contemplation is truly the work of grace. All one can do is to dispose one's self in prayer so as to receive God's Spirit who in turn suffuses all creation with divine love even in the midst of suffering.

Bibliography

Athanasius. *The Life of Antony and the Letter to Marcellinus*. Translated by Robert C. Gregg. New York: Paulist, 1980.

Augustine. *Confessions*. Translated by Henry Chadwick. Oxford University Press, 1998.

Aschenbrenner, George. "Becoming Whom We Contemplate," *The Way Supplement* no. 52 (Spring, 1985) 30–42.

Buckley, Michael. "The Structure of the Rules for the Discernment of Spirits." *The Way Supplement* no. 20 (Autumn 1973) 19–37.

Davis, Leo Donald. *The First Seven Ecumenical Council (325–787): Their History and Theology*. Collegeville, Minnesota: The Liturgical, 1983.

Da Camara, Luis Goncalves. *A Pilgrim's Testament: The Memoirs of St. Ignatius of Loyola*. Translated by Parmananda R. Divarkar. Saint Louis: The Institute of Jesuit Sources, 1995.

Downey, Michael, ed. *The New Dictionary of Catholic Spirituality*. Collegeville, Minnesota: The Liturgical, 1993.

Dunne, Tad. *Lonergan and Spirituality: Towards a Spiritual Integration*. Chicago: Loyola University Press, 1985.

English, John J. *Spiritual Freedom: From an Experience of the Ignatian Exercises to the Art of Spiritual Guidance*. 2nd ed. Chicago: Loyola University Press, 1995.

Feldmeier, Peter. *Christian Spirituality: Lived Expressions in the Life of the Church*. Winona, Minnesota: Anselm Academic, 2015.

Gallagher, Timothy M. *The Discernment of Spirits: An Ignatian Guide for Everyday Living*. New York: Crossroad, 2005.

Ganss, George E., trans. *The Spiritual Exercises of Saint Ignatius of Loyola*. St. Louis: The Institute of Jesuit Sources, 1992.

Hay, David. "Experience." In *The Blackwell Companion to Christian Spirituality*, edited by Arthur Holder, 419–41. Oxford and Malden, MA: Blackwell, 2005.

Hausherr, Irénée. *Penthos: The Doctrine of Compunction in the Christian East*. Translated by Anselm Hufstader. Kalamazoo, Michigan: Cistercian, 1982.

Kadloubovsky, E., and G. E. H. Palmer, trans. *Writings from the Philokalia: On Prayer of the Heart*. London: Faber & Faber, 1979.

King, Ursula. *Christian Mystics: Their Lives and Legacies throughout the Ages*. Malwah: New Jersey: Hidden Spring, 2001.

Kolvenbach, Peter-Hans. *The Road from La Storta*. Edited by Carl F. Starkloff. St. Louis: The Institute of Jesuit Sources, 2000.
LaCugna, Catherine Mowry. *God for Us: The Trinity and Christian Life*. San Francisco: Harper Collins, 1991.
Lonergan, Bernard J. F. *The Subject*. Milwaukee: Marquette University Press, 1968.
———. *Method in Theology*. University of Toronto Press, 1990.
Lubac, Henri de. *The Mystery of the Supernatural*. Translated by Rosemary Sheed (1965). New York: Herder and Herder, 2013.
———. *Catholicism: Christ and the Common Destiny of Man*. Translated by Lancelot C. Sheppard and Sister Elizabeth Englund, OCD. San Francisco: Ignatius, 1988.
Luibheid, Colm, trans. *John Cassian: Conferences*. Classics of Western Spirituality. New York: Paulist, 1985.
Maloney, George. *Prayer of the Heart: The Contemplative Tradition of the Christian East*. Notre Dame, Indiana: Ave Maria, 1981.
May, Gerald G. *Addiction and Grace: Love and Spirituality in the Healing of Addictions*. New York: Harper Collins, 1988.
Merton, Thomas. *New Seeds of Contemplation*. 1961. Reprint, New York: New Directions, 2007.
———. *No Man Is an Island*. 1955. Reprint, San Diego: Harvest, 2002.
Meyendorff, John. *Saint Gregory Palamas and Orthodox Spirituality*. Crestwood, New York: St. Vladimir's Seminary, 1974.
Newman, John Henry. *An Essay in Aid of a Grammar of Assent*. Indiana: University of Notre Dame Press, 2005.
Nguyen, Joseph H. *Apatheia in the Christian Tradition: An Ancient Spirituality and Its Contemporary Relevance*. Eugene, OR: Cascade, 2018.
O'Brien, Elmer, trans. *The Essential Plotinus*. Indianapolis, Indiana: Hackett, 1964.
O'Sullivan, Michael. "Trust Your Feelings, but Use Your Head: Discernment and the Psychology of Decision Making." *Studies in the Spirituality of Jesuits* 22.4 (September 1990) 1–38.
Padberg, John, ed. *Jesuit Life & Mission Today: The Decrees & Accompanying Documents of the 31st–35th General Congregations of the Society of Jesus*. Saint Louis: The Institute of Jesuit Sources, 2009.
Rahner, Karl. *The Trinity*. Translated by Joseph Donceel. New York: Herder and Herder, 1970.
———. *Foundations of Christian Faith*. Translated by William V. Dych. New York: Crossroad, 1978.
———. "Experience of Self and Experience of God." In *Theological Investigations*, translated by David Burke, 13:122–32. New York: Crossroad, 1975.
———. "The Relationship between Nature and Grace: The Supernatural Existential." In *A Rahner Reader*, edited by Gerald McCool, 185–90. New York: Crossroad, 1984.
Rausch, Thomas P. *This is Our Faith: An Introduction to Catholicism*. New York: Paulist, 2014.
Rich, Antony D. *Discernment in the Desert Fathers: Diakrisis in the Life and Thought of Early Egyptian Monasticism*. Colorado Springs: Paternoster, 2007.
Saliers, Don E. *The Soul in Paraphrase: Prayer and the Religious Affections*. Akron: OSL, 1980.
Smiljanic, Ana, trans. *Our Thoughts Determine Our Lives: The Life and Teachings of Elder Thaddeus of Vitovnica*. Saint Herman of Alaska Brotherhood, 2014.

Steiner, Rudolf. *How to Know Higher Worlds*. Translated by Christopher Bamford. 1909. Reprint, Barrington, MA: Anthroposophic, 1994.

Teresa of Avila. *Teresa of Avila, Interior Castle*. In *The Collected Works of Saint Teresa of Avila*, translated by Kieran Kavanaugh and Otilio Rodriguez, 2:##-##. Washington, DC: Institute of Carmelite Studies, 1980.

Toumanova, Nina A., trans. *The Way of a Pilgrim*. Mineola, NY: Dover, 2008.

www.ingramcontent.com/pod-product-compliance
Lightning Source LLC
Chambersburg PA
CBHW070932160426
43193CB00011B/1669